THE DATA PROCESSING SECURITY GAME
Safeguarding Against the Real Dangers of Computer Abuse

ROBERT S. BECKER
IBM General Systems Division

PERGAMON PRESS

New York / Toronto / Oxford / Sydney / Frankfurt / Paris

HF
5548.37
B39
1977

Pergamon Press Offices:

U.S.A.	Pergamon Press Inc., Maxwell House, Fairview Park, Elmsford, New York 10523, U.S.A.
U.K.	Pergamon Press,Ltd., Headington Hill Hall, Oxford OX3, OBW, England
CANADA	Pergamon of Canada, Ltd., 207 Queen's Quay West, Toronto 1, Canada
AUSTRALIA	Pergamon Press (Aust) Pty. Ltd., 19a Boundary Street, Rushcutters Bay, N.S.W. 2011, Australia
FRANCE	Pergamon Press SARL, 24 rue des Ecoles, 75240 Paris, Cedex 05, France
WEST GERMANY	Pergamon Press GmbH, 6242 Kronberg/Taunus, Frankfurt-am-Main, West Germany

Library of Congress Cataloging in Publication Data

Becker, Robert S
    The Data Processing security game.

    Bibliography: p. 100
    1. Electronic data processing departments—— Security measures. I.   Title.
HF5548.2.B36 1977   658.4'7   76-51326
ISBN 0-08-021790-7

Printed in the United States of America

TO MECHTHILD

OTHER PERGAMON TITLES OF INTEREST

Books

Bernstein—*Computers in Public Administration*

Singer & Wallace—*The Administrative Waltz*

Journals

Computers in Biology and Medicine

Computers & Chemical Engineering

Computers & Chemistry

Computer Coupling of Phase Diagrams and Thermochemistry

Computers & Education

Computers & Electrical Engineering

Computers & Fluids

Computers & Geosciences

Computers & Graphics

Computers & The Humanities

Computers & Industrial Engineering

Computers & Mathematics with Applications

Computers & Operations Research

Computers & Structures

Computers & Urban Society

CONTENTS

Preface

PREFACE

What is Data Processing Security?

Data processing security is the protection of an organization's physical assets and assets in computer processable data, as well as the facilities and organizations which handle it. It is, in other words, concerned with the protection of the DP environment—that environment which encompasses DP hardware, software, people, magnetic media, input/output areas, and communication terminals and associated transmission lines.

Background

In the last few years, we have seen the emergence of highly sophisticated complex computer installations. At the same time, we have seen an increase in the use and complexity of shared systems. It is this environment, together with the very nature of the data "housed" within it, that has highlighted the following needs:

- to provide protection for processable data
- to provide protection for the equipment (computer terminals, etc.) handling the data
- to provide protection for the magnetic media on which the data resides
- to provide the legal basis (documentation) required to prosecute an adversary in a court of law;

or, in more general terms,

- to provide a comprehensive data processing (DP) security program

Scope

It is the intent of this book to set forth the fundamental elements required to insure acceptable DP security levels in a business environment. Five major areas of concern (physical aspects, magnetic media control, terminal systems, data set control, and disaster recovery) will be discussed in some detail. In addition, planning recommendations and underlying philosophies will be developed, together with control procedures and associated checklists.

Audience

This text is intended as a ready reference for corporate executives and DP professionals at all levels of the business:

- for corporate and professional DP executives to gain a better understanding of the need for DP security, the ramifications involved, and their role in the DP security game
- for the professional DP manager to gain an insight into the nature of the DP security game, to understand the exposures that may be faced, together with the options available to effectively minimize or eliminate these exposures
- for the DP installation manager to effect a sound DP security program
- for auditing professionals to gain an appreciation of basic DP security requirements
- for college professors to use as an effective reference manual regarding the fundamentals of DP security

Acknowledgments

I should like to take this opportunity to extend my gratitude to the many participating people within the worldwide DP security community for their unselfish contributions to this work. In particular, I would like to thank Mr. Richard C. Cook, Mr. Ivan Gavrilovic, and Mr. Richard B. Morron for their many suggestions and their time in reviewing this book.

I am extremely grateful to my wife for her patience, understanding, and spiritual guidance during my preparation of this book, and to Miss Peggy A. Oliver for her professional typing and editing support.

CHAPTER 1

OVERVIEW

Philosophy

There are several basic philosophical points that I should like to make at the outset of this book. Like any other subject matter, DP security embodies a certain amount of philosophical thinking. The philosophical points which follow formulate the conceptual framework of this text and, as the reader will see, manifest themselves in the many fundamental concepts that will be discussed.

The DP Security Game

DP security is a game. It is a strategy to "out strategize" the potential adversary. To clarify this point, I should like to draw an analogy between the DP security administrator and a football coach, both of whom have a "potential" adversary. The football coach faces a potential adversary weekly during his season. He knows his opponent's identity, mode of operation, and objectives. Using this information, he determines the strengths and weaknesses of his adversary before each weekly encounter. He then establishes a "win" or game plan, which is designed to take advantage of the adversary's weaknesses and attempts to nullify his strengths.

The DP security administrator is in very much the same position except that he is not analyzing his adversary—he is analyzing his DP environment. Through this analysis, he should be attempting to determine his strengths and his weaknesses in order to develop his game plan—a plan to thwart or "out strategize" his potential adversary. Thus, we have the DP security game.

The Defensive Threshold

It must be understood that 100% security (i.e., absolute prevention of penetration) is not attainable. No matter what type of security program one has in place, it can be broken by a determined adversary. The idea is to design a DP security program which will be unpalatable to the potential adversary in terms of his time and money. In other words, it is essential to establish a defensive threshold that is high enough to make the investment in time and money unprofitable to any potential adversary.

Risk Management

Security does cost money. How much, will depend on what there is to protect and how it is to be protected. In this process, one will weigh what is to be protected against the cost of protecting it, together with the possibility and probability of loss, and then decide how much to protect (see Figs. 1-3).[1] In doing so, of course, one will take the risk of not protecting certain elements in the DP security environment and, thus, one will have made a risk/management decision

---

[1]The Diebold Research Program, *Insuring The Security of the Information Resource*, 1971, pp. 58-59.

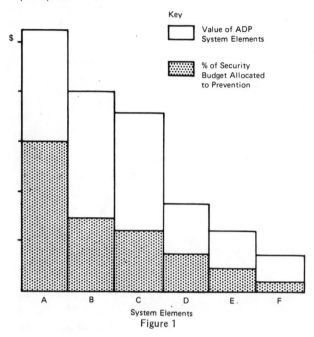

Key

☐ Value of ADP System Elements

▨ % of Security Budget Allocated to Prevention

System Elements

Figure 1

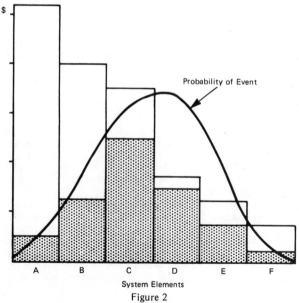

Probability of Event

System Elements

Figure 2

4

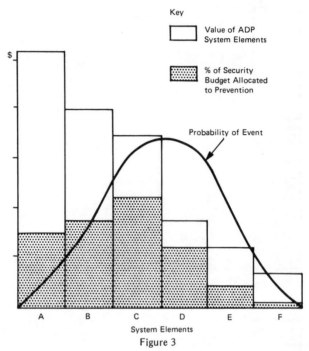

Key

☐ Value of ADP
System Elements

▨ % of Security
Budget Allocated
to Prevention

Probability of Event

$

A   B   C   D   E   F

System Elements

Figure 3

The three graphs on these pages represent three distinct approaches or philosophies as to how the data processing security budget should be allocated.

In the first graph, Fig. 1, the budget is allocated in approximate proportion to the value of the various aspects of the resource; that is, the greatest amount of money goes to protect the most costly elements. This is the *traditional* approach.

As Fig. 2 indicates, however, a different allocation pattern results when the added factor of probability is considered. In Fig. 2 the budget is allocated roughly in proportion to the probability of an attack on a given element of the resource. But the left-hand side of the graph suggests that a substantial high-cost, high-value portion of the resource may be underprotected.

Figure 3 represents an attempt to match the allocation of the security budget to probability, but without disregarding the "high-ticket" elements where a loss, although not likely, could be devastating. This shift of emphasis comes at the expense of protection in the extreme right-hand area, where probability and value both are minimal. In contrast to Fig. 2, however, the high-value elements are protected. This is, in the opinion of The Diebold Research Program, the "optimal" allocation pattern.

Figures 1, 2 and 3 are courtesy of the Diebold Group, Inc.

—a decision to maximize DP security at a reasonable cost.

Selective Protection/Compartmentation
Let's look at some of the alternatives that are available in lieu of 100% protection: among them are selective protection and compartmentation. By selective protection, we mean protecting that which requires protection—for example, new development information, production information, financial information, personnel information, etc. By compartmentation, we are suggesting job organization in the DP environment. Jobs should be so organized that no one individual has the total picture of a sensitive project. Jobs in this sense can be programs, terminal text updates for new development projects, procedural aspects in the handling of financial or personnel information in a computer installation, or program coding of a sensitive program. In other words, through the prudent use of selective protection and compartmentation techniques, one can begin to formulate an acceptable defensive threshold.

Management Involvement—Top Down
The successful DP security program must have management involvement and this involvement must be from the top down as opposed to a "bottom up" approach. The very nature of DP security dictates this approach. DP security can be thought of as an "indirect" activity in that it does not directly impact the development of a product, the manufacture of a product, or the sales or service of a product. At the same time, DP security can be thought of as a "direct" activity—directly impacting the very structure of the business; for the DP community is, in fact, the heart of most businesses today. Unfortunately, in most

corporations and companies today, it is the former point of view that prevails. It is because of this that most organizations find it difficult to initialize a DP security program. To overcome this erroneous perspective and to establish the proper one, it is essential that DP security programs be initiated from top management levels downward through the organization and that they not be allowed to become diluted in the process.

DP Security Program Administrator

Each DP security program should be implemented and maintained under the direction of a DP security administrator. This individual should possess a knowledge of the business with which he is associated, should be a data processing professional, and should be one with personal stature in the organization. Because of the reasons cited in the preceding paragraph, it is essential that this administrator have high organizational visibility. The position must report to a member of executive management in larger firms or be part of an executive's responsibilities in smaller firms.

The DP security administrator should be just that— an administrator. Essentially, this job should coordinate the total DP security program through management at all levels of the business. It is the line manager who must have the ultimate responsibility for implementing and maintaining DP security in his operating unit.

Organization of This Text

A rational systematic approach to DP security is essential to the selection of those security measures required to provide an acceptable DP security program. There is no one program to meet the varied requirements of the multitude of types of DP installations in existence today. Each installation must be considered unique and therefore the DP security program must be tailored to satisfy its particular requirements. It is the intent of this book to set forth the basic elements of an acceptable DP security program which can and should be used by all installations regardless of size, scope, or mission.

In the ensuing chapters, we will discuss what to do and, where applicable, how to do it. Each of the chapters has been set up as a separate entity such that the reader can focus on those subjects which are of prime importance to him in a quick and efficient manner. Each chapter contains a "Summary" which is, in effect, an outline of the chapter.

CHAPTER 2

THE ASSESSMENT

Background

This is where the DP security game really begins. Before one can design and implement an acceptable DP security program, there must be a complete understanding of the firm's DP security posture. The first step, then, in the DP security game is an assessment or self-evaluation of the DP environment. "Assessment involves (1) determining the acceptability of existing safeguards provided by hardware systems, and (2) examining other facets of the security program, such as personnel measures, physical measures, emanation, and communication security." [1] The objective, of course, is to determine the major security strengths and weaknesses in this environment. Once these strengths and weaknesses have been determined, a plan should be developed and implemented to bring the weaknesses to an acceptable level and improve upon the strengths, where that's possible. In this chapter we will discuss the assess-

---

[1] Gerald F. Short, "Establishing A Company Security Program," IBM Data Security Forum, Denver, 1974, p. 8.

ment itself. Succeeding chapters will dwell on recommended security techniques and their implementation within an acceptable DP security program.

Definitions

Before embarking on our discussion of the assessment procedure, it is important that the following terms and their significance in the DP security game are understood:

- computer installations
  - closed computer installations
  - open computer installations
- security classifications
- major exposures

A "computer installation" is construed as *any* room with a central processing unit (CPU) installed. There are generally two types—"closed" and "open."

A "closed computer installation" is characterized by the presence of assigned operators who in effect control machine operation, input/output flow, and to some degree access to the installation. It is "closed" to direct operation by outsiders (programmers, engineers, etc.).

An "open computer installation" is one in which the user himself is operating the equipment. In this environment, then, there is direct user control of system operation and, thus, of any input to or output from that system. The very nature of this environment presents the possibility of unauthorized activities which could be significant security exposures: unmonitored transmission of data, unmonitored copying of data, and unmonitored use of the equipment itself.

"Security classifications" are essential to the fundamental structure of a DP security program. Each
asset within the DP environment—hardware, software,
data sets, magnetic media, hard copy, etc—must be
assigned a security classification by the user/propri-
etor so that each DP asset can be afforded the protection dictated by its classification. Typical classifications are: secret, confidential, and internal use.
(Refer to Chapter 4 for details.) In other words, by
assigning each asset a security classification, we are,
in effect, identifying those assets which we should
be protecting and, through the assessment technique,
insuring that acceptable protection is, in fact, in
place.

The "major exposures" fall into the following
general areas:

- physical access (to installation)
- magnetic volume access
- system software access
- data set access
- open installation exposures
  - unmonitored (unauthorized) copying
  - unmonitored (unauthorized) transmission of data
  - unmonitored (unauthorized) use of equipment
- terminal systems

It is these exposure areas that are analyzed as part
of the DP assessment which we will now discuss.

Implementation Technique

The DP security assessment can be accomplished in a
multitude of ways. I should like to recommend that
it be conducted in two phases, the first at a gross
level to determine the major strengths and weaknesses
and this followed by a second phase to determine the

remaining significant strengths and weaknesses. By using this bi-level technique, immediate focus is placed on the major security exposures which good business sense dictates should be addressed with the highest priority.

As there are many ways to conduct a self-assessment, there are also many tools that can be used to obtain the assessment results. The tool that I have used personally, and that I highly recommend, is the grid analysis technique, which is illustrated in Fig. 4. Both phase one and phase two mentioned above can be easily and quickly accomplished by using this technique. The DP security administrator should assist the installation manager in completing the grid analysis. As you can see in Fig. 4, the various installations are listed vertically in the grid and their related characteristics horizontally on the grid. The characteristics shown in the diagram are considered basic. Others, of course, can be added as required in a given situation. The headings shown beg the following questions which are exactly those that should be asked of the installation manager:

What security classification is most commonly handled in your installation? (column one)

What is the name and location of your installation? (column two)

What is your mission? (column three)

Are you an open or closed installation? (column four)

What is the highest security classification that is handled in your installation? (column five)

What exposures *could* you have? (column six)
- physical access (to installation)
- magnetic volume access
- system software access
- data set access

1	2	3	4	5	6	7	8	9
						Control Requirements		
Installation Security Class	ID	Mission	Installation Type	Security Class	Exposure Types	Access	Account- ability	Residual Exposure
Confiden- tial	Information Systems	Location Support	Closed	Confiden- tial	Magnetic Volume Control	Librarian Volume Labeling	Activity Log	Equipment
					Terminal System Access	Unique ID	Transaction Traceability	
Unclassified	Customer Education	Customer Seminars	Open	Unclassified	Computer Room Access	Locked Doors	Visitor Log	Equipment

Assessment Grid Analysis

Figure 4

- open installation exposures
  - unmonitored (unauthorized) transmission capability
  - unmonitored (unauthorized) copy capability
  - unmonitored (unauthorized) equipment use
- terminal systems

What control requirements should be in place? (columns seven and eight)

- access controls
- accountability controls

What residual exposures remain? (column nine)

After completing the grid on the first pass (phase one), the installation manager should then be in a position to quickly determine where his major security strengths and weaknesses lie. The weaknesses will make themselves manifest through the lack of controls or through deficient controls. It is at this point that the installation manager should begin to develop his plan for improving the deficient controls and/or putting in place those that are lacking. Priority should be given to those areas which present the greatest exposure. The decision of what to protect and to what extent it should be protected will be, as we mentioned earlier, a risk/management decision—one that will be made on the basis of cost versus the value of the items being protected. This, of course, will be different from situation to situation. After phase one is completed and a corrective plan is initiated, the installation manager should, if time and money permit, enter into phase two in the same manner in which he conducted phase one.

In succeeding chapters we will discuss, in addition to planning recommendations and control procedures, the requirements of acceptable:

- physical access control
- magnetic volume control
- data set protection
- terminal systems

Summary

What to Do?
- Understand the security posture of the data processing environment
  - Determine strengths and weaknesses
  - Develop program to eliminate or bring weaknesses to an acceptable level

How to Do It?
- Two phases
  - Phase one—gross analysis
    (determine major strengths and weaknesses)
  - Phase two—follow-on analysis
    (determine other significant strengths and weaknesses)
  - Implement program improvements
- Tools
  - Grid analysis
  - Definition (computer installation, security classification, major exposures)

CHAPTER 3

PHYSICAL ASPECTS

Background

"Physical security is a prerequisite for any security." [1]

There are many basic areas of physical security to be considered in the data processing security game. Among these are computer installations, equipment, magnetic volume control, data set protection, and terminal security. Each of these areas requires certain minimal security control mechanisms and procedures. It is these control mechanisms and procedures that we will discuss. This chapter will focus on the security of the installation, related input/output areas, and equipment. The remaining basic areas will be discussed in subsequent chapters.

Definitions

As a prelude to this chapter, it is important that you understand the following terms:

---

[1] "The Considerations of Physical Security in a Computer Environment," IBM, 1970.

- restricted area
- controlled access
- magnetic volume
- magnetic volume library

Any "restricted area" is construed as an area where access is limited to authorized individuals only (i.e., computer installations, terminals rooms).

The term "controlled access" implies the ability to determine by date and time of day individual access to and egress from a restricted area.

A "magnetic volume" is any computer processable magnetic media (disk, tape, diskette, cassette).

A "magnetic volume library" is construed as either a separate room or cabinet established for the purpose of housing magnetic volumes.

Physical Mechanisms and Procedures

The Installation

As we mentioned earlier, physical security is the prerequisite for any security program. To graphically demonstrate the basic attributes of an acceptable physical security program, we have provided a typical installation layout in Fig. 5.

First and foremost, every computer installation ("open" or "closed"), should be a restricted area. This is to insure that only those people authorized to work in the computer installation are permitted into this environment or, in other words, that all nonauthorized people are denied entry. This serves, then, as the first line of defense in the installation portion of the total DP environment.

In order for this restricted access mechanism to be successful, it is essential that all access to and egress from a restricted area be controlled. How do we

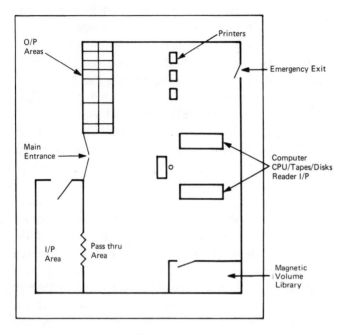

Figure 5

effect restricted access control? The following recommendations attempt to answer this question.

Where practical to do so, each installation should designate one primary entrance through which its normal business is conducted. All other exits should be used for emergency only and should be alarmed and, in some cases, have a visual indicator (flashing light). The primary entrance should be outfitted with either a cypher lock or badge lock (one such available is the IBM* System/7 Control Access System). Various other manufacturers provide similar systems. Procedurally, all visitors (nonauthorized personnel) must be accompanied in, through, and

_____

*Registered Trademark of International Business Machines Corporation.

out of the computer installation and logged in and out of that installation. The most desirable arrangement, of course, is a badge system that will accommodate visitors as well as regular employees. A second option is a combination of the badge lock system and visitor log. Such tracking mechanisms will put total access/egress activity at your fingertips if so required. If an installation were illegally penetrated, this information would be most valuable during the investigative process in an attempt to identify the adversary or intruder.

Installations should be designed so that computer operators or other computer installation personnel in their normal working area have a "view" of the main installation entrance. By "view," we are referring to both a visual and *audible* view of the main entrance. This can be accomplished through the use of strategically placed mirrors and buzzers. These devices, while generally low in cost, could very well enhance the DP security posture by providing the computer installation personnel with a challenge capability (the ability to challenge the entrance of unfamiliar individuals) that otherwise might not have existed. To effect this, of course, operators must be educated accordingly and given the job responsibility to challenge.

Installations should not be designed as groundfloor show cases. Rather, they should be deliberately placed so that they are away from public view. This will provide an added deterrent to those who might be inclined to physically destroy an installation by bombing, grenading, etc.

Input/Output Areas

An integral part of any computer installation is its input and output areas. While it is not absolutely essential, it is preferable to have these areas adjacent to or even a part of the computer installation itself. Control in the input/output areas is especially important with regard to classified information (programs, cards, magnetic volumes, hard copy) and should be the responsibility of an "Installation Control Center." Typically, an installation control center is an area manned by computer personnel and organizationally designed as the computer center interface to its user community.

Input

Classified input (jobs) that are tape, cassette, diskette, or card oriented must be under the discrete control of the computer installation control center. In other words, computer operators should not be starting or actually running such classified jobs without the prior consent of the "Control Center." This same procedure does not hold true in the disk environment, for here we are talking about data set control and this will be discussed in more detail in Chapter 5, which is entitled "System Security."

Magnetic volumes submitted to an installation must be logged in at the time of installation acceptance. Those that are classified must be handled by authorized personnel only. Magnetic volume control will be discussed in more detail in Chapter 4, which is entitled "Magnetic Volume Control."

Output

Classified output in any form (hard copy, magnetic volumes, cards, etc.) must be controlled at all times within the data processing environment. It is the user's or customer's responsibility to exercise similar control outside of the data processing environment. Classified hard copy output should be processed by authorized[2] computer operators selected on the basis of past performance. It should be placed in sealed envelopes and marked with the appropriate security classification. Magnetic volume and/or card output should be marked both externally and internally (labeled) with the appropriate security classification. All classified output should normally be delivered to authorized recipients through the use of a locked output box (mailbox) facility or on a personalized basis. Locked output boxes should be assigned to either authorized individuals or departments as required in a given situation. A master key system with deadbolt locks should be used on the lock boxes and no more than two keys should be issued for any one box. Combination locks should be discouraged because of the ease of transfer of the combination from one individual to another and the obvious difficulty in tracing this act in the event of an incident.

Equipment

Equipment security embraces two basic areas:

- equipment inventory control
- equipment locking mechanisms and procedures

Equipment inventories (machine types, location, and usage) should be taken periodically (preferably monthly) and reconciled to either equipment rental invoices or capitalization schedules. This procedure not only provides equipment control, but it also provides a good financial control by insuring that the billing in any given month is not excessive.

Equipment locking mechanisms (console, I/O gear,

---

[2]AFIPS "System Review Manual on Security," 1974, p. 16.

etc.) are available in the marketplace, but not commonly used. This is one area of potential vulnerability that can be virtually eliminated at very low cost, particularly in the area of computer consoles and permanently mounted disk packs. There are, in addition to those devices offered by equipment manufacturers, suitable inexpensive local approaches that can be employed in a given installation without marring the face of the original equipment or changing the aesthetic look of the installation. Since equipment design differs from manufacturer to manufacturer, it is suggested that each system be reviewed individually. It is, however, highly recommended that lock features offered by manufacturers be considered when ordering their equipment. These security devices could and, in most cases, will raise the security threshold of a particular installation at a very low cost.

General

There are some general considerations in the area of physical installation security. Among these are people's attitudes, installation cleanliness, and emergency /first aid education.

People run computer installations. These people, through their actions and attitudes, determine the effectiveness of computer installation security. It is extremely important, then, to insure that installation personnel are happy and content with their work, understand the need for and procedures applicable to DP security, and are motivated to perform at a level of maximum effectiveness. The converse of this situation could prove to be disastrous. A discontented employee represents a high risk security threat and, as an "insider," is most costly to protect against.

Installation cleanliness is generally a good indicator of the DP security level of a given installation. In other words, the telltale mark of an unsecure installation is an untidy installation. Unfortunately, this is more often true than not and, therefore, if a characteristic of a particular installation, should be of concern to the management in that area.

Emergency/first aid procedures tend more toward the safety rather than the security aspects of a business but because of their importance deserve some mention here. Because of the host of electrical equipment in a computer installation, together with the highly inflammable magnetic media it houses, it makes good business sense to insure that computer installation personnel are schooled in emergency procedures (fire fighting, first aid, etc.), and that appropriate emergency equipment is readily available for their use.

Summary

What to Do?
- Understand the physical requirements regarding the computer installation, equipment, magnetic volume library, and terminal security
- Verify that the proper control mechanisms/procedures regarding the security of the installation, equipment, magnetic volume library, and terminal security are, in fact, in place

How to Do It?
- Review the physical control procedures and mechanisms related to the installation, equipment, magnetic volume library, and terminal security
  - Insure that the computer installation is a restricted area and that a controlled access documentation mechanism is in place

- —Insure that classified input is handled appropriately upon entrance into, through, and exit from the data processing environment
- —Insure that equipment security controls are in place
- Insure that emergency procedures concerning fire and first aid are in place

CHAPTER 4

MAGNETIC VOLUME CONTROL

Background

Magnetic volume control is perhaps one of the most significant areas in the DP security game. The sophisticated adversary is primarily interested in obtaining proprietary information, rather than in the theft, damage, or use of computer equipment. This proprietary information in large part resides on magnetic volumes (tapes, disks, diskettes, cassettes). It is necessary, then, to have in place a security program that will protect magnetic volumes and, in particular, those volumes containing proprietary information from the sophisticated adversary. In this chapter we will address just such a program.

Library Control

Philosophy

Magnetic volumes should reside in a magnetic volume library at all times except when in transit between magnetic volume libraries in an authorized mode. This is basic to effective magnetic volume control.

Legal Implication

The legal implication here is quite important. In order to prosecute an adversary or win damages and restoration of the lost asset in a court of law, it is necessary to prove to the court beyond any reasonable doubt that an effective structured magnetic volume control program was in place at the established time of volume loss.

Structure and Organization

To have acceptable magnetic volume control, the following requisites must be in place:

- a magnetic volume "library" must be established as a separate entity for the purpose of housing all magnetic media
- a librarian responsibility must be assigned to an individual on a full- or part-time basis
- data security classifications must be established and all volumes labeled within this structure
- access and accountability control procedures must be established

The magnetic volume "library" should be either a room, separate from but adjoining the computer installation itself, or merely a cabinet designated for this purpose and residing within the computer installation. The number and types of magnetic volumes will dictate the library structure that is suitable for a given installation. In any case, the library should be suitably locked and fireproofed.[1]

A librarian must be assigned the responsibility for each library which is established. The librarian can

---

[1] James Martin, "Security Accuracy and Privacy in Computer Systems," Englewood Cliffs, N.J. Prentice-Hall, 1973, p. 311.

act in a full-time or part-time capacity depending, of course, on the size and the amount of activity in a given library. The librarian is responsible for volume labeling, access to, and accountability for all volumes.

In order to afford the proper level of protection to each of the magnetic volumes residing in a given library, it is essential that they be classified within some security classification structure that is workable and practical. I recommend no more than three classification levels; perhaps internal use, confidential, and secret or some such naming convention (as mentioned in Chapter 2).

"Internal use" would include information which, because of its nature, should be restricted to use within the company.

"Confidential" would include information sensitive enough to not only be restricted to use within the company but, in addition, to use by selected individuals only.

"Secret" would pertain to information of the highest proprietary value.

To use more than three categories will only increase the complexity of the classification structure and really buy no additional security. In fact, the result will be to make it more difficult to properly classify a particular magnetic volume. Once the security classification structure has been established, it is the responsibility of the owner/proprietor of the data to classify the magnetic volumes that contain his data. It is then the responsibility of the librarian to affix the appropriate security classification label to the volume, file it, and protect it accordingly. When, because of the nature of the data, a magnetic volume requires declassification, it is the responsibility of the owner/proprietor to advise the librarian. The librarian then should relabel the media accordingly.

Access and accountability controls can be both intra and interlibrary in nature. These are discussed in the following sections.

Intralibrary Environment

Access Controls

Two basic access authorization lists are required. The first is a user "need to have" list, which is a list of individuals authorized by appropriate owner/proprietor management to use the volumes which they have indicated. The second is a production run "need to have" list. In this situation, appropriate owner/proprietor management has authorized the use of specified volumes in computer center production runs. Those that are classified confidential or higher (payroll, personnel, accounts payable) should be released only to specifically designated "confidential" operators in the computer installation. These lists, once established, should be reviewed on a periodic basis to insure that they remain in a current status. The owner/proprietor should communicate list updates as they occur and, most importantly, when an employee is transferred or terminated. A special personnel procedure should be in place to trigger this latter action.

Activity Logging

The librarian must formally log the release and return of each magnetic volume. This is important from a business point of view (inventory control) and also in the legal sense (post-incident investigation). It is recommended that a log format as shown in Fig. 6 be used. While the exact format shown is not critical,

Employee Name	Employee Number	Magnetic Badge No.	Volume Numbers	Date Out	Time Out	Date In	Time In	Destination

Magnetic Volume Activity Log

Figure 6

the content is, for it is essential that information recorded be complete enough to support any post-incident investigation that might take place. Therefore, at minimum, the information should include the name of the individual to whom the volumes are released, employee identification number (if any), the numbers and security classification of the volumes released, the data released, the time of day released, and the destination of the volumes. When the volumes are subsequently returned, the "date in" and "time in" columns are completed.

Inventory Control

In addition to access and activity log controls, inventory control is an essential element of any magnetic volume control program. It is essential that the librarian know at all times the whereabouts of all magnetic volumes. Use of the activity log mentioned above will aid the librarian in this effort. To insure that total control of all volumes is in place, an inventory must be taken on some periodic basis. Assuming that we have three security classification levels, internal use, confidential, and secret, we recommend the following inventory intervals:

- secret—at least weekly and more so as required
- confidential—at least monthly
- internal use and unclassified—at least quarterly

The inventories should be formally documented in writing and approved by authorized computer installation management. Any volume loss detected by this inventory, in the confidential or secret classification, should be immediately reported to the DP security administrator for investigation. Should this investigation reveal the need for local law enforcement assistance, this should be sought through normal business channels.

Interlibrary Environment

Library Identification
In order to establish acceptable controls between two or more libraries, it is necessary to identify all existing libraries and then create a list of magnetic volume librarians who have been authorized by the appropriate management areas. Once created, this list must be maintained in a current status. It is recommended that a polling of the various management areas be taken on a monthly basis to satisfy this requirement.

Authorized Transit Between Libraries
As we mentioned earlier, magnetic volumes should reside in a magnetic library at all times, except when in authorized transit between magnetic volume libraries.

The term "authorized transit" implies that the bearer of volumes outside of a magnetic volume library is also the bearer of some formal authorization to carry those volumes in that environment. This formal authorization is normally in the form of a written document (property pass) which contains the volume identification information, the signature of the owner/proprietor, the releasing librarian, and the recipient of the volumes (the bearer himself). While this is a perfectly acceptable approach, I would like to recommend an alternative—the use of a magnetic volume control badge. Such a badge would be issued with the released volumes in lieu of the property pass, and its identification number would be included with the other pertinent information in the activity log we discussed earlier. This provides several direct benefits:

- the property pass paperwork is eliminated
- documentation of all volume activity (one log accommodating all information) is centralized
- a challenge capability outside of the magnetic volume library restricted access area is established

As a result of the challenge capability just mentioned, an indirect benefit is derived. Because of the inherent nature of people to avoid red tape, the badge challenge capability actually tends to influence people to insure that their magnetic volumes are, in fact, resident in a magnetic volume library as opposed to their desks. More often than not they will reside in the volume library that is associated with the computer installation in which the magnetic volumes will ultimately be used.

Other Considerations

In order to maintain the integrity of the magnetic volume control program within the intent of the philosophy mentioned earlier, the mail room, receiving, and shipping areas in addition to the receptionist must be included as check points for magnetic volume activity.

Procedures should be in place in the mailroom and in receiving areas to insure that volumes mailed or shipped to the site are delivered only to authorized librarians, not to any other addressee. By the same token, procedures should be in place in the mail room and shipping areas to insure that volumes mailed or shipped from the site are addressed to bonafide recipient librarians, and mailed only by authorized librarians. Upon receipt of a volume, the librarian should notify the owner.

The receptionist's responsibility is to log in all volumes hand-carried onto the site, issue a badge to provide authorized transit through the site, and then reclaim the badge and log the volume out as it is leaving the site.

Summary

What to Do?

- Establish magnetic volume control philosophy
- Establish library, librarian

How to Do It?

- Develop and publish magnetic volume control policy
- Determine location, number, and types of magnetic volumes
- Create library and associated facilities to store magnetic volumes
- Develop librarian responsibilities
- Assign librarian to carry out responsibilities
- Audit to insure a controlled magnetic volume library posture

CHAPTER 5

SYSTEM SECURITY

Background

The systems security environment today represents a potential area of exposure in the DP security game, one which the industry in general is beginning to address. This exposure has been brought about by the increasingly complex systems that have been introduced into the marketplace, together with the tremendous expansion that has taken place in the Remote Job Entry (RJE) and on-line data base/data communications environment. This very posture becomes more and more palatable to the sophisticated adversary who, as was mentioned earlier, is ever attempting to obtain proprietary information (product strategies, financial condition, customer lists, etc.). It is because of this that an acceptable system security program must be in place. Terminal system security and data base protection are the two basic elements of the systems security program.

Terminal System Security

An acceptable terminal security program must include the following:

- administrative controls
  - assigned system security administrator
- software access controls
  - unique subscription identification
  - unique terminal operator identification
  - unique terminal identification
- investigative (legal) control
  - complete terminal systems use traceability
- systems management responsibility
  - define user security responsibilities
  - cite system security user tools

Administrative Controls

Each terminal system must have a security administrator assigned. The basic responsibilities of this
position should be subscription control and system
security violation investigation.

Subscription control involves the issuance of sub-
scriptions (system access codes) and the maintenance
of the system subscription list. It is recommended
that subscription requests be accepted in writing only
from authorized managers. Further, the request in a
standardized format (See Fig. 7) should include the
following information:

For security
- subscriber's name and employee number
- subscriber's department, office or branch number
- reason for subscription (need and intended use)
- subscriber's manager signature (authorization), department, and phone number

For other
- subscriber's charge account, credit card number,
  or office number charged (accounting information, if required)

Terminal System ID   _____

Authorized Subscriber
  Name   _____
  Employee Number   _____
  Department Number   _____
  Location   _____

Accounting Information
  Charge Code   _____

Space Requirements
  Disk Space
  Number of Cylinders   _____

Reasons for Subscription   _____

                            _____

                            _____

                            _____

Requesting Manager   _____

Department Number   _____

Location   _____

Phone Number   _____

_____   _____
    Authorized Signature   Date

Terminal System Request

Figure 7

- system disk space to be used (operation information, if required)

Procedurally, the receipt of a subscription request should be verified by telephone contact with the requesting manager to insure authenticity of the letter before subscription initialization takes place. Once the subscription is initialized, the system security administrator must confirm this to the requesting manager in writing. This confirmation should include the subscriber's sign-on key (subscription identification and terminal operator identification) together with a list of system security rules that are to be adhered to by the subscriber and an operators guide. (See Fig. 8 and "Systems Management Responsibility" below.)

The subscription list should be reviewed periodically through subscription management to insure its current status. However, a special ongoing personnel procedure should be in place regarding transferred or terminated employees. This procedure must insure that the security administrator is notified immediately upon transfer or termination of an employee. In this way, subscription cancellation can be affected in parallel with the departure of the employee.

System security violation investigation is required to determine first the nature of the violation (intentional or accidental). If intentional, it is through the investigative mechanism that the necessary facts will be accumulated for possible use in the legal arena (prosecution of an identified adversary in a court of law). Both intentional or accidental violations should be brought to the attention of the subscription manager. Accidental violations should be addressed by the subscription manager as deemed necessary.

Terminal System Identification

System Security Capability

 This system is capable of handling company confidential data only.

System Security Rules

 Do not place secret data on this system except in
 compartmentalized form. When this technique is
 used, you must insure that no one document is
 higher than confidential in nature.

 All confidential documents must be password protected.

 All documents considered sensitive in nature regardless of classification must be scrambled.

 All data entered into this system must be classified
 upon entry.

 System security violations are subject to possible
 loss of job and prosecution.

Terminal Security Rules

 All terminals must contain a console locking device.

 All terminals must reside in a locked room.

 All terminal output (if paper oriented) must be
 removed from the terminal by the user after each
 session.

 The user (subscriber) is responsible for the security
 of the unique subscription key issued to him/her.

Terminal Systems Rules

Figure 8

Software Access Controls

The software elements mentioned above (subscription identification, terminal identification, terminal operator identification) are commonly found in terminal systems in use today. Subscription identification relates the user to a particular terminal system. It is, in effect, the key to the system and normally consists of four or five alphanumeric characters. This key customarily is initially assigned by the terminal system security administrator, as mentioned above, and is maintained in a table which is internal to the system. The system in 30-day intervals should either issue a new subscription key or force the user to change to a new key. The original key should be rendered unusable for at least 90 days. This then becomes the first of three software security access screens which should be present within the terminal system environment.

In addition to subscription identification, the system should require a unique terminal operator identification (personal identification of the user). It is recommended that this be a personal characteristic, such as an employee code which is typed into the system or entered into the system through the use of an employee badge or a voice or fingerprint. These alternatives have been addressed by many companies and, as a result, it seems now that the most practical approach is the use of an employee number encoded in an employee badge. As in the case of the subscription identification, a table must be initialized within the system by the security administrator to reflect authorized terminal operators for that particular system.

The third level of access control is unique terminal identification.

While terminal identification is available, a great

many terminal systems today do not employ this control mechanism. What is required is a hardware feature placed on the terminal itself and appropriate software in the terminal operating system which would seek out this signal at the appropriate time (presumably at sign-on). While newer terminals include this function, a great many of the older terminal systems do not have the software to which we have just referred, because at the time these systems were developed security was not a primary consideration. Where a system caters to dial-up terminals (those using conventional telephone lines and equipment), a serious potential exposure exists. Without unique terminal identification, the system really won't know the terminal accessing it and it may very well be residing in a competitor's office. Hence, the need for unique terminal identification. Access control is graphically displayed in Fig. 9.

Investigative (Legal) Control

System use traceability is required to satisfy the legal process—that is, the needs of the investigation and prosecution process. This, again, is a software feature which should provide a record of all system access by subscription identification, operator identification, and terminal identification. It should also record activity by data set transaction (READ, WRITE, UPDATE).

The system use traceability software package should provide a record of all security violations for use by the security administrator as mentioned above under "Administrative Controls." To reiterate, this function (system activity traceability) is key to successful investigation of an attempted penetration, and most importantly is the tool which will provide the hard facts necessary in a court of law during the

44

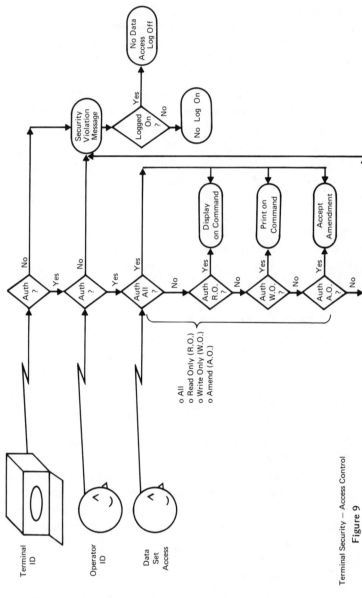

Terminal Security – Access Control

Figure 9

prosecution of an identified adversary. Without this tool, attempts at investigation and prosecution will be exceedingly difficult. Unfortunately, many terminal systems today do not include a system activity traceability software feature.

Systems Management Responsibility

Systems management (the organization offering the terminal service) has an obligation to inform its users of their responsibilities with regard to the use of that particular system and with regard to the physical handling of the terminals themselves.

In the area of system requirements, the systems manager should indicate to the user the highest security level that his particular terminal system is capable of protecting. This can be made abundantly clear to the user not only through the customary letter or memo route but can also be displayed at the terminal by the system each time that an individual signs onto the system. The systems manager should also inform the user of the security tools that are available for his use on a particular terminal system. For example, the availability of a password protection, or scramble (encryption) feature should be made known and their use explained.

The password protection feature allows the user to place a "key" (or shibboleth, if you will) on a given data set. This key is selected and used at the discretion of the user and, therefore, known only to him. I would recommend that all confidential data sets be password protected at the very least.

The scramble "key" renders a data set unintelligible if printed out. In application, scrambling involves the encoding and decoding of data. In other words, a request for a printout of the data set without the use of the proper scramble decode key would result in unrelated symbols and letters in printed form. The scramble technique is recommended for sensitive confidential information and for all secret information.

In the physical terminal area, the systems manager should inform the user of the desired physical terminal environment. He should indicate whether the terminal should bear a console lock and whether the terminal should be maintained in a locked room at all times. In addition, the systems manager should inform the user that it is his (the user's) responsibility to protect his or her subscription key and personal operator identification (passwords and scramble keys) at all times. This information should remain unique to an individual except where, by system design, it is absolutely essential to have subscription identification in a group mode.

Conclusion

Terminal systems have become a way of life in the data processing community in many businesses today. This environment is growing at a rapid pace. As it does, it becomes more and more essential to ensure that adequate security measures are in place. Subscription identification and terminal operator identification are fairly common elements in the terminal systems of today. While many new systems are incorporating this, it should be remembered that many old systems don't have this capability. Terminal identification and terminal use traceability are lacking in a great many systems today. The absence of these two elements renders a terminal system potentially susceptible to penetration by the determined adversary.

Hence, where this situation exists, serious thought should be given to immediate corrective action whether that action involves complete software system replacement or the introduction of additional software into the current system.

Data Set Protection

Background

"Data security is a very large and complex area. It is perhaps where computer security becomes the most technically challenging. At present there is no magic solution on the market. A truly certifiable version of a 'secure' operating system has not yet been provided. However, all major manufacturers are planning for their future systems to meet the requirements of users for truly secure hardware and software."[1]

As indicated above, most system software offerings on the market today do not have the basic built-in security functions required in an acceptable data processing security program. Common to many existing software packages (operating systems) is a password protection feature which is initiated by the user, but not demanded nor monitored by the system and a date protect feature which is exercised by the system. In addition, many systems provide a scramble feature of sorts. These were discussed earlier in this chapter under the section "Systems Management Responsibility."

Operating System Security Requirements

To establish and maintain an acceptable system security posture, a security administrator must be assigned to each operating system.

---

[1]Peter S. Browne, "Computer Security—A Risk Management Approach," Computer Security Institute, First Annual Computer Security Conference and Workshop, New York, 1974, pp. PB-12.

A secure operating system should contain those security functions that control access to and use of data sets, those that control data sets based on their security classification, and those that monitor and record all system access activity and exits. In addition, this system should include a security reporting mechanism.

Access Control
Access control must be authorized at the discretion of the data author. This individual must identify those individuals whom he has authorized to access his data. In addition, he must define the extent of their accessibility in terms of authorized activity (read only, write only, append only).

Data Set Classification
In order to protect the data based on its particular security classification, data classification must be made essential to system acceptance. The system software, then, must be capable of restricting the manipulation and output of all classified data. The level of restriction will be directly related to the level of data classification.

System Traceability
System traceability is required to provide a deterrent to those who might otherwise attempt system penetration and to provide a tool during the investigative stage following a security incident. The tracing function should record all accesses to the system by name, employee number, date, time of day, data set accessed, and type of transaction performed.

As part of the traceability function, the security software system should provide the terminal oriented user with a new sign-on key randomly assigned on a monthly basis or should force the user to change his key on a monthly basis. In either situation the system should require a completely different sign-on key for each 30-day period and limit the reuse of any one sign-on key to 90-day cycles.

Security Violation Report Mechanism

A security report procedure must be included to communicate all access or system's use violations. This report should be directed to the system security administrator for immediate action. Access violations will include all attempts, deliberate or unintentional, to initiate an unauthorized transaction type. System use violations include any deviation from the normal sequencing of sign-on, access, transaction, or sign-off procedures. A violation of any kind should require system reinitialization on the part of the user and job cancellation after the occurrence of two consecutive violations.

System Extensions

Extensions to current operating systems such as the Resource Access Control Facility[2] (RACF), and the Information Management System[3] (IMS) can be employed to obtain some of the functions noted above. IMS, for example, defines the portion of a data base that an application program can access. In addition it controls the type of access (Get, Insert, Delete, Replace) and records this activity.

Administrative Requirements

There are administrative procedures and standards

---

[2] IBM Corporation, "Resource Access Control Facility (RACF)," G520-3081.

[3] IBM Corporation, "IMS/VS General Information Manual," GH20-1260.

which should be implemented to strengthen the defensive threshold. Administratively, we are alluding to the concept of compartmentation—the breaking down of highly confidential data sets into pieces which are, by themselves, less than confidential in nature. By "standards," we are talking about initiating system procedural conventions which dictate that the user use password protection on such data sets as we have just described and, where necessary and available, scramble keys. When initialized, these procedures will provide three levels of security that did not otherwise exist and, while not foolproof, will substantially raise the level of the defensive threshold.

Conclusion
The basic requirements of an acceptable and secure data set protection system have been discussed above. These characteristics will not only provide a reasonably high defensive threshold, but at the same time will provide the traceability ingredient that is required for protection in the legal environment. In the absence of these characteristics, the data set protection mechanism stands exposed and, in the case of an incident, the ability to trace and prosecute an adversary is almost nonexistent.

Summary

Terminal Systems
What to Do?
- Establish terminal security requirements
- Administrative controls
  - Assign system security administrator
  - Define responsibilities
- Software access controls
  - Unique subscription identification

        —Unique terminal operator identification
        —Unique terminal identification
- Investigative (legal) control
        —System use traceability
- Systems management responsibility
        —Define user security responsibility
        —Cite system security user tools

How to Do It?

- Administrative controls
        —Select an individual as terminal system security administrator
- Software access controls
        —Review terminal system software to insure access controls mentioned above are operational; if a control is missing, consider the addition of coding to provide it, or system replacement
- Investigative (legal) control
        —Review terminal system software to insure that a system use traceability feature is operational; if missing, consider the addition of coding to provide it or system replacement
- Systems management responsibility
        —Set up standardized formats for:
          subscription requests
          system user security requirements and tools

Data Set Protection
What to Do?

- Establish a system security administrator
- Define responsibility
- Establish operating system security requirements
        —Process controls
        —Data set classification
        —System traceability
        —Security violation report mechanism

- Establish administrative requirements

How to Do It?

- Select an individual as system security administrator
- Review system software to insure access controls mentioned above are operational; if a control is missing, consider the addition of coding to provide it, or system software replacement
- Review administrative requirements and effect changes required.

CHAPTER 6

BACKUP PROCEDURE

Background

An acceptable data processing security program is not complete without a formalized backup procedure (disaster/recovery plan) in place. This is essential to insure the integrity of the business environment and the security environment at all times. The elements of an acceptable backup procedure together with recommended implementation plans are discussed below.

Backup Procedure Elements

The following are the basic elements to be considered in a backup procedure program:

- alternative hardware (backup machine)
- alternative system software (backup system software)
- off-site stored vital magnetic media and associated run documentation
- trained personnel
- identified organization interfaces
  - intracompany

- intercompany
- formalized written instructions
  - detailed procedures
  - assigned responsibility
  - test procedures

Locating a backup system and negotiating for its availability will be for the large firm a not so arduous task, but for the small firm it may very well be a frustrating task. Alternative hardware similar in configuration to the system to be backed up must be located at some other physical location. Companies that have several computer installations, spread out geographically, will undoubtedly seek an alternative within the confines of their own company. On the other hand, single installation businesses should look to other business organizations for their backup hardware. Computer manufacturer sales representatives can be a very useful source in this matter since they can direct a customer to other customers with similar hardware configurations. Many computer manufacturers will offer this service upon request. The arrangement, when finalized, should be mutually beneficial to the parties involved. Each of the two installations should look to the other as its alternative, and all the necessary arrangements should be made accordingly and agreed to in writing.

In addition to system hardware, system software must be compatible in the backup location. Because operating systems are generally not identical from one location to the other, software bridges will have to be built between the two systems.

In order to insure a current data posture, it is essential that magnetic media be stored off-site on a periodic basis. Storage frequency will depend on the volatility of data and the ability to recover it if lost.

We recommend that vital magnetic media (media critical to the business operation) be stored on a weekly basis in an off-site location, together with the run documentation that supports the use of that media. By doing this, an installation would be subject to a maximum of one week loss of data.

A recovery procedure involves not only the hardware, the systems software, and the media in the data processing environment, but most importantly it involves the people who will carry out the task. It is essential, therefore, that personnel be selected to carry out this disaster/recovery task and then be trained to do this job. Personnel should be selected from both the original and alternate sites to carry out the disaster/recovery plan.

Once the hardware, software, media, and personnel have been tended to, the next order of business will be to develop procedures to reconstruct the vital files for the various internal areas of the business. It will be necessary to establish interfaces to these areas for this initial task and also for any intracompany activity that may be required during an actual recovery process. In addition to these intracompany interfaces, intercompany interfaces will, in all probability, be necessary. Generally, in a disaster/recovery area the local power company, telephone company, and DP forms suppliers will play a vital role in the recovery process. It is, therefore, highly recommended that these organizations be contacted and interfaces be included in the total backup procedure.

The total backup procedure must be documented in a formal set of written instructions. These instructions should include a detailed step-by-step procedure which, if properly implemented, will effect total recovery in the shortest possible time. In addition, this document should indicate the manager responsible for backup plan execution and periodic review. Universal terminology should be used (as opposed to terminology unique to a particular computer installation) so that personnel at the alternate site could, if necessary, reconstruct the original installation from its set of instructions. It is recommended that this procedure be reviewed semi-annually and updated as required.

Once all of the basic elements of a disaster/ recovery plan are in place, the total plan should be tested. Without a test, there is no way of knowing whether the plan itself actually works. In this test bugs will be found in your original procedural setup that will need correction.

While a full-blown test would be time consuming and costly, to say the least, an abbreviated test of the backup procedure is in order. The test should be pre-planned with the alternate location and predicated on the assumed loss of: certain data sets or perhaps total volumes containing various data sets, associated run documentation, some personnel and equipment. With those assumptions clearly stated, the backup procedure as formally documented should be invoked. Essentially this will include:

- initial notification to all parties concerned including the alternative site
- retrieval of backup media and run documentation at the selected off-site storage facility
- centralization of the backup procedure team at the alternative site to implement the recovery program as prescribed by the formal set of instructions

Through the use of a proven set of backup instructions, and assuming that alternative hardware and software are immediately available, disaster recovery should take place within a relatively short period of time. A suggested disaster/recovery plan outline is shown below.

Disaster/Recovery Plan Outline

I. Objective
   A. Reconstruction of existing computer center service levels within a reasonable time frame (to be established by each installation)
II. Assumptions
   A. Equipment, software, and backup time requirements
   B. Personnel involved and organization structure
   C. Alternate location
   D. Written agreement
III. Procedures
   A. Disaster notification
       1. Own location
          a. Intracompany
          b. Intercompany
       2. Alternate site
       3. Magnetic media storage facility
   B. Restoration/Initialization
       1. Restoration team instructions
          a. Restore operating system disk packs or tapes (identified in a separate list).
          b. Restore data sets for vital applications (identified in a separate list).
   C. Scheduling/Processing
       1. Plan manual scheduling of vital applications
       2. Input—identify sources (key departments, individuals, other DP systems, keypunch, teleprocessed, etc.)
       3. Output—delivery and pickup procedures

58

IV. Replacement
  A. Hardware
    1. Detail listing of current configuration
    2. Manufacturers contact to effect replacement
  B. Software
    1. Identify documentation source
      a. Identify retrieval procedure for the above

Conclusion

The disaster/recovery program is a necessary entity in the DP security game. Because of its importance in the conduct of running a business, it is essential that it be formulated and tested before the disaster occurs. To attempt to formulate a disaster/recovery program during the disaster would be disastrous in itself.

Summary

What to Do?
- Establish backup procedure elements
  - Alternate hardware
  - Off-site magnetic storage facility
  - Personnel
  - Contacts
    - intracompany
    - intercompany
  - Formalized written instructions
  - Test (instructions)

How to Do It?
- Place management responsibility for backup procedure program
- Alternate hardware

- —With manufacturers representatives determine alternative locations available
- —Reach mutual agreement with one to provide backup for one another
- Alternate system software
  - —System support personnel should review alternate site system and provide necessary software bridges (if required)
- Off-Site magnetic media storage facility
  - —Investigate and select a suitable off-site location for the storage of vital magnetic media *and* related run documentation
- Personnel
  - —Select personnel to carry out backup plan and train
- Contacts (intracompany, intercompany)
  - —Identify contacts in each major intracompany organization
  - —Identify contacts required outside of the company (telephone company, power company)
- Formalized written instructions
  - —Write formalized step-by-step backup procedure
- Test
  - —Test backup procedure (semi-annually)
  - —Update as required

CHAPTER 7

CONTROL ASPECTS
AND BUSINESS CONSIDERATIONS

Control Aspects

In the preceding chapters we have described the basic elements involved in the establishment of an acceptable DP security program. Once these pieces of the program are in place, it will be necessary to initiate a mechanism to insure the continuation of the acceptable posture established. The control mechanism recommended is an audit program.

The audit control program is a many-faceted program. If performed properly, it will involve individuals at various levels throughout the organization ranging from the computer installation technician up to and including the corporate internal auditor.

What is involved in an audit control program? Essentially, what is required is a comprehensive audit checklist for each of the areas of the DP security program. The use of this list should provide a reasonable test of the control mechanism that is in place or point out lack of control, as the case may be. It should, therefore, be directed to the meaningful control points in the DP security program. In this way it will be easy to use and will provide a relatively quick means of determining installation security control posture at any time.

The properly developed audit control checklist will be usable at any level in the organization. That is to say, it will not be so grossly stated that it cannot be used at the installation level and at the same time it would not be in such detail that it cannot be used at the corporate level. From the point of view of consistency of program operation, it is essential that each level of the business use the same audit control checklist, for in this way all players are playing the same game by the same set of rules. To play the DP security game in any other way is sheer folly.

Data Processing Security Audit Checklist

This section contains a DP security audit checklist which meets the objectives stated above. It is designed to test the many control areas in the DP security program and in addition is designed for ease of use by the auditor at whatever level of the business he or she may be.

Background

This DP security audit checklist is organized parallel to the organization of this text. Except for the initial section of this checklist, each of the sections relates directly to a particular chapter referenced at the beginning of each section of this checklist.

Audit Checklist

	Yes/No	Comments

I. Organization Requirements

A. Is management aware of the need for DP security programs and aware of its responsibilities regarding this program?

B. Are written data processing procedures in place?

C. Is there a data processing security administrator?

D. Are the data processing security administrator's responsibilities defined in writing?

E. Does the data processing security administrator have a data processing security audit program in place?

F. Has a data processing security assessment and/or audit been performed in the last year?

G. Have the assessment/audit problem areas been suitably addressed?

II. Physical Aspects (Chapter 3)

A. Is the computer installation a restricted area?

B. Is there visitor logging at the primary entrance of the computer installation?

C. Are all secondary entrances alarmed?

D. Are mounted classified volumes locked when unattended?

Yes/No   Comments

E. Is equipment inventoried monthly and reconciled to rental invoices and/or capitalization schedules?

F. Is all classified input externally marked or labeled with the appropriate security classification?

G. Is all classified output externally marked or labeled with the appropriate security classification?

H. Is all classified information (hard copy, magnetic volumes, etc.) handled properly entering into, through, and going out of the data processing environment?

I. Is the data processing environment maintained in an orderly fashion?

J. Are blank forms (certificates, blank checks, etc.) properly controlled?

K. In an open computer installation, are the exposures in the following areas at an acceptable level:
- unmonitored (unauthorized) transmission capability
- unmonitored (unauthorized) copy capability
- unmonitored (unauthorized) equipment use

III. Magnetic Volume Control (Chapter 4)

A. Is the magnetic volume library a separate locked facility within the computer installation restricted area?

Yes/No   Comments

B. Is there a full-time or part-time
librarian assigned?

C. Are all magnetic volumes
uniquely identified?

D. Are all magnetic volumes externally labeled with the security
classification of the data they
bear?

E. Are all magnetic volumes normally resident within the computer installation restricted area
except when in transit in an
authorized mode outside of
that area?

F. Are magnetic volume releases
for use outside the computer
installation restricted area
properly documented?

G. Is the release of classified magnetic volumes controlled?

H. Are magnetic volumes inventoried on a periodic basis?

I. Is this inventory documented?

J. Is there an acceptable written
control procedure for classified
volumes?

IV. System Security (Chapter 5)
Terminal System Security

A. Does each remote terminal
system uniquely identify each
user?

B. Does each remote terminal
system uniquely identify each
terminal?

66

Yes/No   Comments

C. Does each remote terminal system insure that security access codes are changed at least monthly?

D. Does each remote terminal system control and monitor (document) user access to and activity with all data sets?

E. Does each remote terminal system require the user when entering or displaying data to state the data classification?

F. Is there a terminal system security administrator for each remote terminal system?

G. Are remote terminal systems subscriptions controlled and maintained by the terminal system administrator?

H. Have the systems managers of each of the remote terminal systems established security standards and procedures for that system?

I. Are the remote terminal system security standards and procedures published and distributed to the appropriate user community?

J. Is the user community audited for compliance with the remote terminal system standards and procedures?

Yes/No   Comments

Data Set Protection

A. Does the operating system provide data set password protection?

B. Does the operating system provide a data set scramble capability?

C. Does the operating system monitor data set access?

D. Does the operating system trace data set transaction activity?
   - by data set name
   - by transaction
   - by day and time of day
   - by user and ID

E. Is there a system security administrator formally assigned?

F. Does the operating system provide a violation activity report for the system security administrator?
   - by access violations
   - by system use violations

G. Are classified data sets password protected?

H. Are classified data sets protected by a scramble key when considered sensitive?

I. Is the compartmentalization technique employed with regard to classified data sets?

Yes/No   Comments

V. General (Chapters 4-7)

A. Does the employee exit or transfer program provide for a DP security sign off?

B. Does the DP security sign-off procedure prior to employee exit or transfer include:

- subscription change (terminal systems)
- password change (data sets)
- check for outstanding magnetic volumes
- removal from need-to-have list (documents and magnetic media)
- removal from computer installation authorization access lists
- employee manager confirmation of all of the above in writing

Business Considerations

DP security is a business. It is the business of protecting the DP environment within reasonable cost limitations. As a business, DP security will involve risk/management decisions—decisions that are predicated on what there is to protect; decisions that will weigh asset value and loss probability against additional cost to protect.

Cost Elements

Yes, DP security does cost money. However, the amount of money spent on such programs will be determined upon what there is to protect and the level of protection that is desired. It will involve certain one-time costs. These may include the cost of additional hardware. They may include the installation of additional software features which will involve machine use cost and programmer cost. They may also involve physical costs such as the cost for additional furniture in the magnetic volume libraries when setting them up, or they may include the cost of the installation of an access control mechanism to a computer installation or installations. These are but a few of the one-time costs that may be involved in the installation of a data security program.

In addition to the one-time costs of DP security, there will be an ongoing or fixed cost for the administration of such a program. The major expense will be the cost of the data processing administrator who will initialize and maintain the program. In addition, costs will be incurred for full- or part-time magnetic volume librarians and for a data set security administrator, both of which (responsibilities) will be employed even in the most minimum DP security environment.

Where terminal systems are installed, there will be a cost for the terminal systems security administrator who is required to initialize terminal systems sub-scriptions and follow through on system security violations (refer to Chapter 5, "System Security").

Another cost element to be considered is the cost of DP insurance. Special policies are written today for the DP environment. They include coverage for losses due to fire and/or flood and lost revenue. Since each installation and its surrounding DP environment is a unique entity, it is recommended that the insurance representative serving your company be consulted for more information on this subject. A typical policy is shown in Appendix III.

While generally the costs noted above are those that will normally be incurred, there could of course be others depending on the nature and the need of a particular installation. The point to remember, however, is that the amount of money to be spent on DP Security will be a direct function of what there is to protect and how it is to be protected.

Summary
Control Aspects
What to Do?
- Establish a control mechanism
  - DP security audit responsibility
  - Audit checklist

How to Do It?
- Assign DP security audit responsibility
- Create DP security audit checklist
  - Use "DP Security Audit Checklist" provided above as a base
  - Add on additional questions as required
- Test checklist by using and modifying as required

Business Considerations
What to Do?
- Determine one-time and ongoing cost elements
- Decide what to protect and how to protect it

How to Do It?
- Review elements of cost and dollarize them
  - Assets (hardware, software, furniture)

—Administrators
- Make risk/management security "go-no go" decision
  —Based on asset value, cost of protection, and current probability of loss

CLASSROOM QUESTIONS

I. Organization Requirements (Chapters 1 and 2)

A. What is meant by "the DP security game"?

B. What is management's role in the DP security game?

C. What is the role of the DP security administrator?

D. Organizationally, where should the DP security administrator reside and why?

E. What is the DP security assessment? What is the intent of this assessment?

F. What is data processing security?

G. What is the legal basis for a DP security program?

H. Is 100% security truly attainable? Please discuss.

I. What is risk/management decision making?

II. Physical Aspects (Chapter 3)

A. Define a computer installation and the types that exist.

B. Define the terms:
- restricted area
- controlled access
- magnetic volume
- magnetic volume library

C. Discuss the statement that "physical security is a requisite for any security program."
D. Name three major open installation exposures and explain each.

III. Magnetic Volume Control (Chapter 4)
A. Discuss the basic business and legal reasons for magnetic volume control.
B. Discuss the basic characteristics of acceptable magnetic volume control.
C. Propose an interlibrary magnetic volume control procedure.

IV. System Security (Chapter 5)
Terminal System Security
A. Name the characteristics of an acceptable remote terminal security program.
B. What is the greatest exposure existing today in the remote terminal security area?
C. What are the system manager's responsibilities with respect to the user community?
D. What is the user community responsibility with respect to a particular remote terminal system?
E. How often should terminal system access codes be changed?
Data Set Protection
A. What are the common protection features available in most operating systems today and how do they offer protection?
B. What is the significance of access control?
C. Discuss the characteristics of acceptable system traceability, its need, and legal ramifications.
D. What is an access violation?
E. What is a system use violation?
F. What is the significance of a violation reporting system?

V. Backup Recovery Program (Chapter 6)

A. Discuss the hardware requirements of the backup recovery program.

B. Discuss the software requirements of a backup recovery program.

C. Discuss the personnel requirements of a backup recovery program.

D. Discuss the media requirements of a backup recovery program.

E. Discuss the instruction requirements of a backup recovery program.

F. Discuss the nature of a backup recovery program test and the reasons for this.

G. Why a backup recovery program?

VI. Control Aspects and Business Considerations (Chapter 7)

A. Explain what is meant by a risk/management decision.

B. To what extent should we protect assets?

C. DP security costs money. Explain.

D. Discuss the term "selective protection."

E. Of what significance is the audit procedure?

F. By whom should audits be administered? How often?

G. What is an audit checklist and of what should it be comprised?

VII. General

A. What are the component areas of a data processing security program?

B. Of the components, which are the more critical? Explain.

C. Explain the importance of data processing security in the government domain.

D. Explain the importance of data processing security in the public domain.

E. Who is ultimately responsible for security?
F. Is data processing security necessary?

SAMPLE FORMALIZED
DP SECURITY ASSESSMENT

Installation DP Security Analysis

Installation Description

ID: Data Processing   Manager: A. G. Smith

Address: Room 527
        743 Hacienda Blvd.
        San Francisco, Calif.

Mission: Basic on-line support of ABC and XYZ
        Terminal Systems

        Administrative Support

            Personnel
            Accounting (Billing, Accounts Receivable, etc.)
            Inventory Control
            Sales Analysis

        New Product Development Support

Manufacturing Support

Major Applications:
Batch
Applications programming development
Order entry
On-Line
ABC System
XYZ System

DP Equipment:
CPU's (Type and quantity):   370/155 (3), Sys/3
Mod 15
I/O: Disk, Tape, Printer, Card Reader Diskette

Installation Exposures/Action Analysis

Guideline Standard	Exposure	Plan/Deviation
Physical Page 2, Para 3	Weak access control monitoring	Investigating several access control sys- tems and procedures —targeted installation 2nd quarter
Physical Page 3, Para 1	I/O control on confidential	Reviewing procedures to insure acceptable controls are in place —targeted implemen- tation 1st quarter
Magnetic Volume Control Page 1, Para 1	No librarian assigned	Will assign individual within 30 days

Magnetic Volume Control Page 2, Para 1	Inventory control lax	Will assign responsibility to librarian when selected
Magnetic Volume Control Page 2, Para 3	Unattended on-line disk packs	Reviewed and concluded risk is low level since room is locked at all times and data is "system scattered" throughout the 50 packs randomly—no action planned

Installation Application Analysis

Identification: Ledger System

Description: The primary purpose of the ledger system is to provide the business with a current reflection of all business financial accounts.

Data Sources
and Classification: Ledger input from Financial Department
         (Confidential)
     Ledger data files (tape) created and stored in data processing
         (Confidential)

Data Output
(Disposition and
Classification):   Ledger print files (tape) created and stored in data processing
         (Confidential)
     Ledger hardcopy to user lock box for pickup
         (Confidential)

80

System/Program
Data Access
Control: Confidential files (tape) released only to
                      authorized individuals (activity logged)

                      System/Program requires uniquely
                      identified files (those mentioned above)
                      for ledger run

Run Frequency: Weekly

Programming
Controls and
Classification:
   Documentation: Ledger program documentation is main-
                      tained in the data processing program
                      documentation room
                              (Internal Use)
   Programs: All ledger source programs are stored off-
                      site on backup magnetic media each week.
                              (Internal Use)

Exposures: NONE

Action Plan: NONE

A TYPICAL DATA PROCESSING INSURANCE POLICY

MULTIPLE PERIL POLICY

PLEASE READ YOUR POLICY

Executive Offices   150 William St., New York, N. Y.

The Company in which this policy is written is an affiliate of the Royal-Globe Insurance Companies. The Companies are under a common ownership and their fire, casualty and marine operations are conducted on a combined basis as a fully intergrated organization.

All the Companies have been established in the United States for many years — four of them having already passed the 100-year mark.

With over 125 offices throughout the United States, the Royal-Globe organization has established a long-standing reputation for service efficiency.

PLANNED
and
EXECUTED
BY

 Welcome to a distinguished family of business policyholders who are insured in one of the oldest and largest insurance organizations in the world.

Thank you for selecting us to protect your insurable interests.

APPLICATION FOR DATA PROCESSING POLICY

NAME OF APPLICANT (INCLUDE NAMES OF ALL SUBSIDIARIES)

BUSINESS ADDRESS

NATURE OF BUSINESS		EFFECTIVE DATE	TERM

RATING INFORMATION

LOCATION	CONTENTS FIRE RATE	COINS. %	E.C. RATE	COINS. %	V. & M. M. RATE	COINS. %
1.						
2.						
3.						

THE APPLICANT HAS THE OPTION of insuring only data processing equipment, or data processing media, or extra expense or business interruption, or may elect to take any two, three or four of the coverages. If desired, the applicant may also purchase these coverages on a deductible basis subject to a minimum deductible of $1,000.00.

DATA PROCESSING EQUIPMENT: The applicant has the option of insuring all or only part of the equipment, which may be either owned or leased, on an actual cash value basis or on a retail replacement cost basis.

ACTIVE DATA PROCESSING MEDIA: The applicant has the option of (1) specifically scheduling items or groups by types, establishing per-unit agreed values, or (2) blanketing all or unscheduled items into a total single value.

DATA PROCESSING EQUIPMENT
(Attach schedule or list below under "Additional Information")

LOCATION	LIMIT OF LIABILITY	OWNED OR LEASED	ACTUAL CASH VALUE	REPLACEMENT COST
1.	$		$	$
2.	$		$	$
3.	$		$	$

VALUATION   ☐ Actual Cash Value   ☐ Replacement Cost*   COINSURANCE   ☐ 80%   ☐ 90%   ☐ 100%   DEDUCTIBLE   ☐ No   ☐ Yes $

DATA PROCESSING MEDIA

LOCATION	LIMIT OF LIABILITY	OWNED OR LEASED	ACTUAL CASH VALUE	REPLACEMENT COST
1.	$		$	$
2.	$		$	$
3.	$		$	$

LIMIT OF LIABILITY (WHILE IN TRANSIT AND WHILE TEMPORARILY WITHIN OTHER PREMISES) $ DEDUCTIBLE APPLICABLE TO DATA PROCESSING MEDIA   ☐ No   ☐ Yes $

EXTRA EXPENSE

AGREED "PERIOD OF RESTORATION"	ESTIMATED EXTRA EXPENSE TO BE INCURRED FOR THAT PERIOD	DEDUCTIBLE
	$	☐ No ☐ Yes $

BUSINESS INTERRUPTION

NUMBER OF "WORK DAYS"**	AMOUNT OF INSURANCE	MEASURE OF RECOVERY	DEDUCTIBLE
Per Week $	$	Per Day	☐ No ☐ Yes $

ADDITIONAL INFORMATION

* Replacement cost must be written with 100% coinsurance.

** Work Day covers a period of 24 hours and means a day on which the operations of the applicant are usually performed.

X68071 – (7/66)   (Continued-Over)

MACHINE CHARACTERISTICS, OPERATION AND EXPOSURES

	YES	NO		YES	NO
ARE ANY MACHINES ENCLOSED IN COMBUSTIBLE MATERIAL OR ARE PANELS LINED WITH COMBUSTIBLE INSULATION OR SOUND DEADNERS?	☐	☐	IS TAPE STORAGE (OTHER THAN TAPE IN USE):		
			☐ IN VAULT		
IS THIS INSTALLATION IN A SPECIAL ROOM, HEREIN AFTER REFERRED TO AS "THE ROOM"?	☐	☐	☐ IN COMPUTER ROOM		
ARE COMPUTERS EQUIPPED WITH VACUUM TUBES?	☐	☐	☐ IN COMBUSTIBLE RACKS		
			☐ IN APPROVED METAL CONTAINER IN A 2-HOUR SAFE		
DOES ANY MACHINE CABLE OR WIRING OUTSIDE OF ROOM PASS THROUGH AREAS CONTAINING COMBUSTIBLE MATERIAL?	☐	☐	WHAT KIND OF TAPES ARE USED?		
			☐ METAL		
ARE ALL UNITS INSIDE THE ROOM GOVERNED BY A MASTER SWITCH?	☐	☐	☐ PLASTIC		
LOCATED; ☐ IN THE ROOM ☐ OUTSIDE THE ROOM			☐ PAPER		
ARE MANUFACTURER'S ENGINEERS PERMANENTLY ASSIGNED TO THE ROOM?	☐	☐	IS FLAMMABLE SOLVENT USED FOR TAPE ROLLER OR CAPSTAN CLEANING?	☐	☐
IS THE ENGINEER'S WORKSHOP INSIDE THE ROOM?	☐	☐	IS SOLVENT KEPT IN 6-OZ SIZE CANS WITH SPOUT ON END?	☐	☐
HAVE DEFINITE ARRANGEMENTS BEEN MADE FOR THE USE OF SUBSTITUTE FACILITIES ELSEWHERE IN THE EVENT OF A SHUTDOWN?	☐	☐	IS FLAMMABLE SOLVENT KEPT IN GLASS BOTTLE?	☐	☐

AIR CONDITIONING EQUIPMENT

	YES	NO		YES	NO
IS ELECTRIC PRECIPITRON PROVIDED IN AIR STEAM TO ROOM?	☐	☐	SCREENED WITH ¼ IN. OR HEAVIER GALVANIZED MESH?	☐	☐
IS ROOM AIR CONDITIONED?	☐	☐	OVER ADJOINING BUILDINGS OR OVER ANY COMBUSTIBLE MATERIAL OR SUBJECT TO SMOKE FROM NEARBY (150 FT.) STACKS?	☐	☐
ARE DUCT LININGS COMBUSTIBLE?	☐	☐			
ARE COMBUSTIBLE FILTERS USED?	☐	☐	DOES SYSTEM HAVE CONTROL SWITCH IN ROOM OR ELECTRIC EYE OR OTHER AUTOMATIC SHUTDOWN SWITCH?	☐	☐
ARE FILTERS OIL-DIPPED?	☐	☐			
IS COMPRESSOR IN ROOM OR IMMEDIATELY ADJOINING?	☐	☐	IS THERE ANY PROVISION FOR DUPLICATION IN EVENT OF SYSTEM SHUTDOWN?	☐	☐
IS FREON USED AS REFRIGERANT?	☐	☐			
IS FRESH OR MAKE-UP AIR INTAKE:					
WITHIN 10 FT. OF THE GROUND?	☐				

WATER DAMAGE

	YES	NO		YES	NO
IS ROOM SUBJECT TO ACCUMULATION OF WATER FROM ITS OWN LEVEL?	☐	☐	ARE FLOOR(S) AND ROOF OVER ROOM WATER-TIGHT TO PREVENT ENTRY FROM ABOVE?	☐	☐
DO WATER LINES OTHER THAN SPRINKLER SYSTEM ENTER OR PASS THROUGH ROOM OR CEILING SPACE?	☐	☐	ARE THERE SPRINKLERED AREAS OVER ROOM?	☐	☐
DO STEAM LINES, OTHER THAN RADIATOR BRANCH LINES FOR COMPUTER ROOM, ENTER OR PASS THROUGH ROOM?	☐	☐	IF ROOM IS SPRINKLERED, ARE COMPUTERS FITTED WITH INCOMBUSTIBLE CANOPIES TO PREVENT ENTRY OF WATER FROM OVERHEAD?	☐	☐

COLLAPSE

	YES	NO		YES	NO
			ARE COMBUSTIBLE FLOORS ABOVE OR BELOW ROOM (EXCL. PEDESTAL FLOOR)?	☐	☐
ARE THERE UNPROTECTED METAL SUPPORTS (POSTS OR BEAMS) ABOVE OR BELOW ROOM?	☐	☐			
			ARE THERE SPRINKLERS ABOVE OR BELOW ROOM?	☐	☐

FIRE

	YES	NO		YES	NO
IS ROOM OF COMBUSTIBLE MATERIAL OR OF ANY MATERIAL ON COMBUSTIBLE STUDS OR SUPPORTS?	☐	☐	IS ANY REPAIR WORK DONE IN ROOM REQUIRING:		
			☐ USE OF FLAME OR FLAMMABLE LIQUIDS		
IS ROOM NEAR OPEN COURTS OR STAIRWAYS OR IN VERTICAL FLUE-WAY, OR RECEIVING OR DELIVERY DOCK OR PORT OR ADJACENT TO PASSAGEWAY?	☐	☐	☐ STORAGE OF FLAMMABLE LIQUIDS		
DOES ROOM HAVE PEDESTAL FLOOR?	☐	☐	IS ROOM EQUIPPED WITH SMOKE DETECTORS?		
			ARE WINDOWS OF ROOM ON AN OUTSIDE WALL?	☐	☐
IS PEDESTAL FLOOR OF COMBUSTIBLE MATERIAL?	☐	☐	IF SO, DO THEY OVERLOOK OR FACE:		
DOES ROOM CONTAIN COMBUSTIBLE CURTAINS OR DRAPES?	☐	☐	☐ A STREET WITHIN 15FT. OF GROUND LEVEL?		
			☐ OTHER BUILDINGS, MATERIALS OR STRUCTURES?		
IS ROOM CEILING OF COMBUSTIBLE MATERIAL OR ON COMBUSTIBLE SUPPORTS?	☐	☐	EXPOSURE:		
IS SMOKING PERMITTED IN ROOM OR IN ADJOINING REPAIR SHOP?	☐	☐	☐ NONE		
			☐ LIGHT		
DO WATCHMAN'S RECORDED ROUNDS TAKE HIM TO ROOM WHEN ROOM IS NOT OPERATING?	☐	☐	☐ MEDIUM		
			☐ SEVERE		
ARE ADEQUATE CARBON DIOXIDE EXTINGUISHERS AVAILABLE IN ROOM?	☐	☐			
ARE GAS MASKS AVAILABLE FOR ROOM?					

DUPLICATE PROGRAM TAPES

	YES	NO		YES	NO
ARE DUPLICATE PROGRAM TAPES MAINTAINED?	☐	☐	ARE THEY STORED IN FIREPROOF VAULT OR SAFE?	☐	☐
			ARE THEY STORED IN A BUILDING RATED AS A SEPARATE FIRE RISK?	☐	☐

NAME OF COMPANY		DATE

AGENT	AGENCY AT

CO. SYM.	POLICY NUMBER	PRODUCER CODE (14)		DATA PROCESSING POLICY	BKR / LOC / REG / BOR / G/A	QW POLICY SYMBOL & NUMBER
	QW					

PROD. NAME ▶		RENEWS OR REPL. POLICY NO.	REPLACED BY POL. NO.	

NAME OF COMPANY _____	**A Capital Stock Insurance Company** herein called the Company

The insurance afforded is only with respect to such and so many of the following Insuring Agreements as are indicated by ☒. The limit of this Company's liability shall be as stated herein, subject to all the terms of this Policy having reference thereto.

NAME AND ADDRESS OF INSURED					
			SUM INSURED	RATE	PREMIUM
POLICY PERIOD: From _____ to _____ At noon Standard Time at place of issuance as to each of said dates.					

☐ 1. **DATA PROCESSING SYSTEM EQUIPMENT:**

LIMITS OF LIABILITY (PARAGRAPH 3)

	IN THE AMOUNT OF		LOCATED AT
A. On Property of the Insured	1	$	
	2	$	
B. On Property leased, rented or under the control of the Insured	1	$	
	2	$	
C.		$	while in transit and while temporarily within other premises.

VALUATION (PARAGRAPH 6) | COINSURANCE CLAUSE (PARAGRAPH 7) | DEDUCTIBLE (PARAGRAPH 8)

☐ A. Actual Cash Value Clause   ☐ B. Replacement Cost Clause   ☐ A. ____ %   ☐ B. 100% $ ____

☐ 2. **DATA PROCESSING MEDIA:**

LIMITS OF LIABILITY (PARAGRAPH 3)

	IN THE AMOUNT OF		LOCATED AT
A. On Property of the Insured	1	$	
	2	$	
B.		$	while in transit and while temporarily within other premises.

VALUATION (PARAGRAPH 6)

A. SPECIFIED ARTICLES	LIMITS OF EACH	LIMITS OF INSURANCE
	$	
	$	
B. ALL OTHERS		$
$	DEDUCTIBLE (Paragraph 7)	

☐ 3. **EXTRA EXPENSE: SUBJECT OF INSURANCE AND PERILS INSURAD (Paragraph 1)**

AMOUNT OF INSURANCE	MEASURE OF RECOVERY (PARAGRAPH 2)	DEDUCTIBLE (PARAGRAPH 8)
$	$	$

☐ 4. **BUSINESS INTERRUPTION: SUBJECT OF INSURANCE AND PERILS INSURED (Paragraph 1)**

AMOUNT OF INSURANCE	MEASURE OF RECOVERY (PARAGRAPH 2)	DEDUCTIBLE (PARAGRAPH 8)
$	$	$

In States where required, the statutory fire conditions are made a part of this Policy.

CHECKED FOR			UNDERWRITING DEPT.			INSPEC- TION	AUDIT
TYPING	CODING	FILING	CURRENT POLICY APPROVAL	RENEWAL RENEW	DECLINE		

EXTRA COPY

In consideration of the payment of premium, this Company does insure the Insured named in the Declarations subject to all of the terms and conditions of this Policy including all of the terms and conditions of the Declarations and Insuring Agreement(s) which are made a part thereof.

GENERAL POLICY CONDITIONS AND EXCLUSIONS

UNLESS PHYSICALLY DELETED BY THE COMPANY OR UNLESS SPECIFICALLY REFERRED TO IN THE INSURING AGREE-MENT(S), THE FOLLOWING CLAUSES SHALL BE PARAMOUNT AND SHALL SUPERSEDE AND NULLIFY ANY CONTRARY PRO-VISIONS OF THE INSURING AGREEMENT(S).

1. **GENERAL CONDITIONS**
   A. TERRITORIAL LIMITS: This Policy insures only while the property is at locations and while in transit within and between the forty-eight contiguous states of the United States of America, the District of Columbia and Canada, unless otherwise endorsed.
   B. REMOVAL: Such insurance as is afforded by this Policy applies while the property insured is being removed to and while at place of safety because of imminent danger of loss, damage or expense and while being returned from such place, provided the Insured gives written notice to this Company of such removal within ten days thereafter.
   C. OTHER INSURANCE: If there is available to the Insured or any other interested party any other insurance which would apply in the absence of this Policy, the insurance under this Policy shall apply only as excess insurance over such other insurance.
   D. ASSIGNMENT: Assignment of interest under this Policy shall not bind the Company until its consent is endorsed hereon; if, however, the Insured shall die, or shall be adjudged bankrupt or insolvent and written notice is given to the Company within sixty days after the date of such adjudication, this Policy shall cover the Insured's legal representative as insured; provided that notice of cancellation addressed to the Insured named in this Policy and mailed to the address shown in this Policy shall be sufficient notice to effect cancellation of this Policy.
   E. MISREPRESENTATION AND FRAUD: This Policy shall be void if the Insured has concealed or misrepresented any material fact or circumstance concerning this insurance or the subject thereof or in any case of any fraud, attempted fraud or false swearing by the Insured touching any matter relating to this insurance or the subject thereof, whether before or after a loss.
   F. NOTICE OF LOSS: The Insured shall as soon as practicable report to this Company or its agent every loss or damage which may become a claim under this Policy and shall also file with the Company or its agent within ninety (90) days from date of loss

a detailed sworn proof of loss. Failure by the Insured to report the said loss or damage and to file such sworn proof of loss as hereinbefore provided shall invalidate any claim under this Policy for such loss.

G. SETTLEMENT OF LOSS: All adjusted claims shall be paid or made good to the Insured within thirty days after presentation and acceptance of satisfactory proofs of interest and loss at the office of this Company. No loss shall be paid or made good if the Insured has collected the same from others.

H. SUE & LABOR: In case of loss or damage, it shall be lawful and necessary for the Insured, or his or their factors, servants and assigns, to sue, labor and travel for, in and about the defense, safeguard and recovery of the property insured hereunder, or any part thereof, without prejudice to this Insurance; nor shall the acts of the Insured or this Company, in recovering, saving and preserving the property insured in case of loss or damage, be considered a waiver or an acceptance of abandonment, to the charge whereof this Company will contribute according to the rate and quantity of the sum herein insured.

I. SUIT: No suit, action or proceeding for the recovery of any claim under this Policy shall be sustainable in any court of law or equity unless the same be commenced within twelve (12) months next after discovery by the Insured of the occurrence which gives rise to the claim. Provided, however, that if by the laws of the State within which this Policy is issued such limitation is invalid, then any such claims shall be void unless such action, suit or proceeding be commenced within the shortest limit of time permitted by the laws of such State.

J. SUBROGATION: In the event of any payment under this Policy the Company shall be subrogated to all the Insured's rights of recovery therefor against any person or organization and the Insured shall execute and deliver instruments and papers and do whatever else is necessary to secure such rights. The Insured shall do nothing after loss to prejudice such rights.

K. APPRAISAL: If the Insured and the Company fail to agree as to the amount of loss, each shall, on the written demand of either, made within sixty (60) days after receipt of proof of loss by the Company, select a competent and disinterested appraiser, and the appraisal shall be made at a reasonable time and place. The appraisers shall first select a competent and disinterested umpire, and failing for fifteen days to agree upon such umpire, then, on the request of the Insured or the Company, such umpire shall be selected by a judge of a court of record in the county and state in which such appraisal is pending. The appraisers shall then appraise the loss, and failing to agree shall submit their differences to the umpire. An award in writing of any two shall determine the amount of loss. The Insured and the Company shall each pay its chosen appraiser and shall bear equally the expenses of the umpire and the other expenses of appraisal. The Company shall not be held to have waived any of its rights by any act relating to appraisal.

L. EXAMINATION UNDER OATH: The Insured shall submit, and so far as is within his or their power shall cause all other persons interested in the property and employees to submit, to examinations under oath by any persons named by the Company, relative to any and all matters in connection with a claim and subscribe the same; and shall produce for examination all books of account, bills, invoices, and other vouchers or certified copies thereof if originals be lost, at such reasonable time and place as may be designated by the Company or its representatives, and shall permit extracts and copies thereof to be made.

M. AUTOMATIC REINSTATEMENT: Any loss hereunder shall not reduce the amount of the Policy.

N. DEBRIS REMOVAL: This Policy is extended to cover expenses incurred in the removal of all debris of the damaged property insured hereunder which may be occasioned by loss caused by any of the perils insured against in this Policy. In no event shall the additional coverage granted by this paragraph increase the Limit of Liability specified in the "Declarations".

O. CANCELLATION: This Policy may be cancelled by the Insured by mailing to the Company written notice stating when thereafter such cancellation shall be effective. This Policy may be cancelled by the Company by mailing to the Insured at the address shown in this Policy written notice stating when not less than ten (10) days thereafter such cancellation shall be effective. The mailing of notice as aforesaid shall be sufficient proof of notice and the effective date of cancellation stated in the notice shall become the end of the policy period. Delivery of such written notice either by the Insured or by the Company shall be equivalent to mailing.

If the Insured cancels, earned premiums shall be computed in accordance with the customary short rate table and procedure. If the Company cancels, earned premiums shall be computed pro rata. Premium adjustment may be made at the time cancellation is effected and, if not then made, shall be made as soon as practicable after cancellation becomes effective. The Company's check or the check of its representative mailed or delivered as aforesaid shall be a sufficient tender of any refund of premium due to the Insured.

P. CONFORMITY TO STATUTE: Terms of this Policy which are in conflict with the statutes of the State wherein this Policy is issued are hereby amended to conform to such statutes.

2. **PERILS EXCLUDED:** This Policy does not insure against loss, damage or expense caused directly or indirectly by:

A. (1) Hostile or warlike action in time of peace or war, including action in hindering, combating or defending against an actual impending or expected attack, (a) by any government or sovereign power (de jure or de facto), or by any authority maintaining or using military, naval or air forces; or (b) by military, naval or air forces; or (c) by an agent of any such government, power, authority or forces;

(2) Any weapon of war employing atomic fission or radioactive force whether in time of peace or war;

(3) Insurrection, rebellion, revolution, civil war, usurped power, or action taken by governmental authority in hindering, combating or defending against such an occurrence, seizure or destruction under quarantine or Customs regulations, confiscation by order of any government or public authority, or risks of contraband or illegal transportation or trade;

B. Nuclear reaction or nuclear radiation or radioactive contamination, all whether controlled or uncontrolled and whether such loss be direct or indirect, proximate or remote, or be in whole or in part caused by, contributed to, or aggravated by the peril(s) insured against in this Policy; however, subject to the foregoing and all provisions of this Policy, direct loss by fire resulting from nuclear reaction or nuclear radiation or radioactive contamination is insured against by this Policy.

THIS POLICY IS MADE AND ACCEPTED SUBJECT TO THE FOREGOING STIPULATIONS AND CONDITIONS, together with such other provisions, agreements or conditions as may be endorsed hereon or added hereto; and no officer, agent or other representative of this Company shall have power to waive or be deemed to have waived any provision or condition of this Policy unless such waiver, if any, shall be written upon or attached hereto, nor shall any privilege or permission affecting the insurance under this Policy exist or be claimed by the Insured unless so written or attached.

IN WITNESS WHEREOF, this Company has executed and attested these presents; but this Policy shall not be valid unless countersigned on the Declarations Page by a duly authorized Agent of the Company.

Corporate Secretary   President/U. S. Manager

This Policy is not complete unless a Declarations Page is attached.

INSURING AGREEMENT
Data Processing System Equipment

1. **PROPERTY COVERED:** Data processing systems including equipment and component parts thereof owned by the Insured or leased, rented or under the control of the Insured, all as per schedule(s) on file with this Company.
2. **PROPERTY EXCLUDED:** This Insuring Agreement does not insure:
    A. Active data processing media which is hereby defined as meaning all forms of converted data and/or program and/or instruction vehicles employed in the Insured's data processing operation;
    B. Accounts, bills, evidence of debt, valuable papers, records, abstracts, deeds, manuscripts, or other documents;
    C. Property rented or leased to others while away from the premises of the Insured.
3. **LIMITS OF LIABILITY:** See "DECLARATIONS".
4. **PERILS INSURED:** This Insuring Agreement insures against all risks of direct physical loss or damage to the property covered, except as hereinafter provided.
5. **PERILS EXCLUDED:** This Insuring Agreement does not insure against loss, damage or expense caused directly or indirectly by:
    A. Damage due to mechanical failure, faulty construction, error in design unless fire or explosion ensues, and then only for loss, damage, or expense caused by such ensuing fire or explosion;
    B. Inherent vice, wear, tear, gradual deterioration or depreciation;
    C. Any dishonest, fraudulent or criminal act by any Insured, a partner therein or an officer, director or trustee thereof, whether acting alone or in collusion with others;
    D. Dryness or dampness of atmosphere, extremes of temperature, corrosion, or rust unless directly resulting from physical damage to the data processing system's air conditioning facilities caused by a peril not excluded by the provisions of this Insuring Agreement;
    E. Short circuit, blow-out, or other electrical disturbance, other than lightning, within electrical apparatus, unless fire or explosion ensues and then only for loss, damage or expense caused by such ensuing fire or explosion;
    F. Actual work upon the property covered, unless fire or explosion ensues, and then only for loss, damage, or expense caused by such ensuing fire or explosion;
    G. Delay or loss of market;
    H. War risks or nuclear risks as excluded in the Policy to which this Insuring Agreement is attached.
6. **VALUATION:**
    A. ACTUAL CASH VALUE—The following clause shall apply if indicated in the "Declarations": This Company shall not be liable beyond the actual cash value of the property at the time

any loss or damage occurs and the loss or damage shall be ascertained or estimated according to such actual value with proper deduction for depreciation, however caused, and shall in no event exceed what it would then cost to repair or replace the same with material of like kind and quality.

B. REPLACEMENT COST—The following clause shall apply if indicated in the "Declarations": This Company shall not be liable beyond the actual retail replacement cost of the property at the time any loss or damage occurs and the loss or damage shall be ascertained or estimated on the basis of the actual cash retail replacement cost of property similar in kind to that insured at the place of and immediately preceding the time of such loss or damage, but in no event to exceed the limit of liability stipulated in the "Declarations".

7. **COINSURANCE CLAUSE:**

A. The following clause shall apply if indicated in the "Declarations": This Company shall be liable in the event of loss for no greater proportion thereof than the amount hereby insured bears to the percent indicated in the "Declarations" of the actual cash value of all property insured hereunder at the time such loss shall happen.

B. The following clause shall apply if indicated in the "Declarations": This Company shall be liable in the event of loss for no greater proportion thereof than the amount hereby insured bears to the percent indicated in the "Declarations" of the actual cash retail replacement cost of all property insured hereunder at the time such loss shall happen.

8. **DEDUCTIBLE:** Each and every loss occurring hereunder shall be adjusted separately and from the amount of each such loss when so adjusted the amount indicated in the "Declarations" shall be deducted.

9. **DIFFERENCE IN CONDITIONS:** It is a condition of this Insurance that the Insured shall file with this Company a copy of any lease or rental agreement pertaining to the property insured hereunder insofar as concerns the lessors' liability for loss or damage to said property, and coverage afforded hereunder shall be only for the difference in conditions between those contained in said lease or rental agreement and the terms of this Insuring Agreement. The Insured agrees to give this Company thirty days notice of any alteration, cancellation or termination of the above mentioned lease or rental agreement pertaining to the lessors' liability.

All other terms and conditions of the Policy not in conflict herewith remain unchanged.

INSURING AGREEMENT
Data Processing Media

1. **PROPERTY INSURED:** Active data processing media, being property of the Insured or property of others for which the Insured may be liable.
2. **PROPERTY EXCLUDED:** This Insuring Agreement does not insure accounts, bills, evidences of debt, valuable papers, records, abstracts, deeds, manuscripts or other documents except as they may be converted to data processing media form, and then only in that form, or any data processing media which cannot be replaced with other of like kind and quality.
3. **LIMITS OF LIABILITY:** See "DECLARATIONS".
4. **PERILS INSURED:** This Insuring Agreement insures against all risks of direct physical loss or damage to the property covered, except as hereinafter provided.
5. **PERILS EXCLUDED:** This Insuring Agreement does not insure against loss, damage, or expense resulting from or caused directly or indirectly by:
   A. Data processing media failure or breakdown or malfunction of the data processing system including equipment and component parts while said media is being run through the system, unless fire or explosion ensues and then only for the loss, damage or expense caused by such ensuing fire or explosion;
   B. Electrical or magnetic injury, disturbance or erasure of electronic recordings, except by lightning;
   C. Dryness or dampness of atmosphere, extremes of temperature, corrosion, or rust unless directly resulting from physical damage to the data processing system's air conditioning facilities caused by a peril not excluded by the provisions of this Insuring Agreement;
   D. Delay or loss of market;
   E. Inherent vice, wear, tear, gradual deterioration or depreciation;
   F. Any dishonest, fraudulent or criminal act by any Insured, a partner therein or an officer, director or trustee thereof, whether acting alone or in collusion with others;
   G. War risks or nuclear risks as excluded in the Policy to which the Insuring Agreement is attached.
6. **VALUATION:** The limit of this Company's liability for loss or damage shall not exceed:
   A. As respects property specifically described in the "Declarations", the amount per article specified therein, said amount being the agreed value thereof for the purpose of this insurance;
   B. As respects all other property, the actual reproduction cost of the property; if not replaced or reproduced, blank value of media; all subject to the applicable limit of liability stated in the "Declarations".

7. **DEDUCTIBLE:** Each and every loss occurring hereunder shall be adjusted separately and from the amount of each loss when so adjusted the amount indicated in the "Declarations" shall be deducted.

8. **DEFINITIONS:** The term "active data processing media", wherever used in this contract, shall mean all forms of converted data and/or program and/or instruction vehicles employed in the Insured's data processing operation, except all such UNUSED property, and the following

_____ ,

(insert names of media not to be insured)

which the Insured elects not to insure hereunder.

All other terms and conditions of the Policy not in conflict herewith remain unchanged.

INSURING AGREEMENT
Extra Expense

1. **SUBJECT OF INSURANCE AND PERILS INSURED:** This Insuring Agreement insures against the necessary Extra Expense, as hereinafter defined, incurred by the Insured in order to continue as nearly as practicable the normal operation of its business, immediately following damage to or destruction of the data processing system including equipment and component parts thereof and data processing media therefor, owned, leased, rented or under the control of the Insured, as a direct result of all risks of physical loss or damage, but in no event to exceed the amount indicated in the "Declarations".

This Insuring Agreement is extended to include actual loss as covered hereunder, sustained during the period of time, hereinafter defined, (1) when as a direct result of a peril insured against the premises in which the property is located is so damaged as to prevent access to such property or (2) when as a direct result of a peril insured against, the air conditioning system or electrical system necessary for the operation of the data processing equipment is so damaged as to reduce or suspend the Insured's ability to actually perform the operations normally performed by the data processing system.

2. **MEASURE OF RECOVERY:** If the above described property is destroyed or so damaged by the perils insured against occurring during the term of this Insuring Agreement so as to necessitate the incurrence of Extra Expense (as defined in this Insuring Agreement), this Company shall be liable for the Extra Expense so incurred, not

exceeding the actual loss sustained, for not exceeding such length of time, hereinafter referred to as the "period of restoration", commencing with the date of damage or destruction and not limited by the date of expiration of this Insuring Agreement, as shall be required with the exercise of due diligence and dispatch to repair, rebuild, or replace such part of said property as may be destroyed or damaged.

This Company's liability, during the determined period of restoration, shall be limited to the declared amount per period of time indicated in the "Declarations" but in no event to exceed the amount of insurance provided.

3. **EXTRA EXPENSE DEFINITION:** The term "Extra Expense" wherever employed in this Insuring Agreement is defined as the excess (if any) of the total cost during the period of restoration of the operation of the business over and above the total cost of such operation that would normally have been incurred during the same period had no loss occurred; the cost in each case to include expense of using other property or facilities of other concerns or other necessary emergency expenses. In no event, however, shall this Company be liable for loss of profits or earnings resulting from diminution of business, nor for any direct or indirect property damage loss insurable under Property Damage policies, or for expenditures incurred in the purchase, construction, repair or replacement of any physical property unless incurred for the purpose of reducing any loss under this Insuring Agreement not exceeding, however, the amount in which the loss is so reduced. Any salvage value of property so acquired which may be sold or utilized by the Insured upon resumption of normal operations, shall be taken into consideration in the adjustment of any loss hereunder.

4. **EXCLUSIONS:** It is a condition of the insurance that the Company shall not be liable for Extra Expense incurred as a result of:

   A. Any local or State ordinance or law regulating construction or repair of buildings;

   B. The suspension, lapse or cancellation of any lease, license, contract or order;

   C. Interference at premises by strikers or other persons with repairing or replacing the property damaged or destroyed or with the resumption or continuation of the Insured's occupancy;

   D. Loss or destruction of accounts, bills, evidences of debt, valuable papers, records, abstracts, deeds, manuscripts or other documents except as they may be converted to data processing media form and then only in that form;

   E. Loss of or damage to property rented or leased to others while away from the premises of the Insured;

   F. Error in machine programming or instructions to machine;

   G. Inherent vice, wear, tear, gradual deterioration or depreciation;

H. Any dishonest, fraudulent or criminal act by any Insured, a partner therein or an officer, director or trustee thereof, whether acting alone or in collusion with others;

I. Damage due to mechanical failure, faulty construction, error in design unless fire or explosion ensues, and then only for loss, damage, or expense caused by such ensuing fire or explosion;

J. Short circuit, blow-out, or other electrical disturbance, other than lightning, within electrical apparatus, unless fire or explosion ensues and then only for loss, damage or expense caused by such ensuing fire or explosion;

K. Delay or loss of market;

L. War risks or nuclear risks as excluded in the Policy to which this Insuring Agreement is attached.

5. **RESUMPTION OF OPERATIONS:** As soon as practicable after any loss, the Insured shall resume complete or partial business operations of the property herein described and, in so far as practicable, reduce or dispense with such additional charges and expenses as are being incurred.

6. **INTERRUPTION BY CIVIL AUTHORITY:** Liability under this Insuring Agreement is extended to include actual loss as covered hereunder, sustained during the period of time, not exceeding two weeks, when as a direct result of a peril insured against, access to the premises in which the property described is located is prohibited by order of civil authority.

7. **DEFINITIONS:** The term "Normal" wherever used in this contract shall mean: The condition that would have existed had no loss occurred.

8. **DEDUCTIBLE:** Each and every loss occurring hereunder shall be adjusted separately and from the amount of each such loss when so adjusted the amount indicated in the "Declarations" shall be deducted.

All other terms and conditions of the Policy not in conflict herewith remain unchanged.

INSURING AGREEMENT
Business Interruption

1. **SUBJECT OF INSURANCE AND PERILS INSURED:** This Insuring Agreement covers against loss resulting directly from necessary interruption of business as a direct result of all risk of physical loss or damage from any cause (except as hereinafter excluded) to the following property owned, leased, rented or under the control of the Insured:

A. Data processing systems, computer systems or other electronic control equipment including component parts thereof;

B. Active data processing media meaning all forms of converted data and/or program and/or instruction vehicles employed in the Insured's data processing or production operation except the following _____

which the Insured elects not to insure hereunder.

This Insuring Agreement is extended to include actual loss as covered hereunder when as a direct result of a peril insured against the premises in which the property is located is so damaged as to prevent access to such property.

2. **MEASURE OF RECOVERY:** In the event such loss or damage results in either a total or partial suspension of business then this Company shall be liable:
   A. for the amount stated in the "Declarations" for each working day during the period of such total suspension of business; or
   B. in the event of partial suspension, for such proportion of the amount stated in the "Declarations" for each working day of total production which would have been obtained during the period of partial suspension had no damage occurred;

commencing with the date of damage or destruction, and not limited by the expiration date of this Insuring Agreement, as would be required through the exercise of due diligence and dispatch to rebuild, repair or replace such described property as has been damaged or destroyed but in no event to exceed the amount of insurance provided.

3. **RESUMPTION OF OPERATIONS:** It is a condition of this insurance that if the Insured could reduce the loss resulting from the interruption of business,
   A. by complete or partial resumption of operation of the property herein described, whether damaged or not, or
   B. by making use of other property at the location(s) described herein or elsewhere, or
   C. by making use of stock at the location(s) described herein or elsewhere, such reduction shall be taken into account in arriving at the amount of loss hereunder.

4. **EXPENSE TO REDUCE LOSS:** This Insuring Agreement also covers such expenses as are necessarily incurred for the purpose of reducing any loss under this Insuring Agreement (except expense incurred to extinguish a fire), but in the absence of prior authorization by this Company or its adjuster, NOT EXCEEDING THE AMOUNT BY WHICH THE LOSS UNDER THIS POLICY IS THEREBY REDUCED.

5. **INTERRUPTION BY CIVIL AUTHORITY:** This Insuring Agreement is extended to include the actual loss as covered hereunder during the period of time, not exceeding two consecutive weeks, when, as a direct result of the peril(s) insured against, access to the premises described is prohibited by order of civil authority.

6. **EXCLUSIONS:** It is a condition of the insurance that the Company shall not be liable for Total or Partial suspension incurred as a result of:

A. Any local or State ordinance or law regulating construction or repair of buildings;

B. The suspension, lapse or cancellation of any lease, license, contract or order;

C. Interference at premises by strikers or other persons with repairing or replacing the property damage or destroyed or with the resumption or continuation of the Insured's occupancy;

D. Loss or destruction of accounts, bills, evidences of debt, valuable papers, records, abstracts, deeds, manuscripts or other documents except as they may be converted to data processing media form and then only in that form;

E. Loss of or damage to property rented or leased to others while away from the premises of the Insured;

F. Error in machine programming or instructions to machine;

G. Inherent vice, wear, tear, gradual deterioration or depreciation;

H. Any dishonest, fraudulent or criminal act by any Insured, a partner therein or an officer, director or trustee thereof, whether acting alone or in collusion with others;

I. Damage due to mechanical failure, faulty construction, error in design unless fire or explosion ensues, and then only for loss, damage, or expense caused by such ensuing fire or explosion;

J. Short circuit, blow-out, or other electrical disturbance, other than lightning, within electrical apparatus, unless fire or explosion ensues and then only for loss, damage or expense caused by such ensuing fire or explosion;

K. Delay or loss of market;

L. War risks or nuclear risks as excluded in the Policy to which this Insuring Agreement is attached.

7. **WORK DAY:** The words "work day", however modified, whenever used in this Insuring Agreement shall be held to cover a period of twenty-four hours and shall mean a day on which the operations of the Insured are usually performed.

8. **DEDUCTIBLE:** Each and every loss occurring hereunder shall be adjusted separately and from the amount of each such loss when so adjusted the amount indicated in the "Declarations" shall be deducted.

All other terms and conditions of the Policy not in conflict herewith remain unchanged.

1 **Concealment,**   This entire policy shall be void it, whether
2 **fraud.**   before or after a loss, the insured has wil-
3   fully concealed or misrepresented any ma-
4 terial fact or circumstance concerning this insurance or the
5 subject thereof, or the interest of the insured therein, or in case
6 of any fraud or false swearing by the insured relating thereto.
7 **Uninsurable**   This policy shall not cover accounts, bills,
8 **and**   currency, deeds, evidences of debt, money or
9 **excepted property.** securities; nor, unless specifically named
10   hereon in writing, bullion or manuscripts.
11 **Perils not**   This Company shall not be liable for loss by
12 **included.**   fire or other perils insured against in this
13   policy caused, directly or indirectly, by: (a)
14 eneмy attack by armed forces, including action taken by mili-
15 tary, naval or air forces in resisting an actual or an immediately
16 impending enemy attack; (b) invasion; (c) insurrection; (d)
17 rebellion; (e) revolution; (f) civil war; (g) usurped power; (h)
18 order of any civil authority except acts of destruction at the time
19 of and for the purpose of preventiлg the spread of fire, provided
20 that such fire did not originate from any of the perils excluded
21 by this policy; (i) neglect of the insured to use all reasonable
22 means to save and preserve the property at and after a loss, or
23 when the property is endangered by fire in neighboring prem-
24 ises; (j) nor shall this Company be liable for loss by theft.
25 **Other Insurance.**   Other insurance may be prohibited or the
26   amount of insurance may be limited by en-
27 dorsement attached hereto.
28 **Conditions suspending or restricting insurance. Unless other-**
29 **wise provided in writing added hereto this Company shall not**
30 **be liable for loss occurring**
31 (a) while the hazard is increased by any means within the con-
32 trol or knowledge of the insured; or
33 (b) while a described building, whether intended for occupancy
34 by owner or tenant, is vacant or unoccupied beyond a period of
35 sixty consecutive days; or
36 (c) as a result of explosion or riot, unless fire ensue, and in
37 that event for loss by fire only.
38 **Other perils**   Any other peril to be insured against or sub-
39 **or subjects.**   ject of insurance to be covered in this policy
40   shall be by endorsement in writing hereon or
41 added hereto.
42 **Added provisions.** The extent of the application of insurance
43   under this policy and of the contribution to
44 be made by this Company in case of loss, and any other pro-
45 vision or agreement not inconsistent with the provisions of this
46 policy, may be provided for in writing added hereto, but no pro-
47 vision may be waived except such as by the terms of this policy
48 is subject to change.
49 **Waiver**   No permission affecting this insurance shall
50 **provisions.**   exist, or waiver of any provision be valid,
51   unless granted herein or expressed in writing
52 added hereto. No provision, stipulation or forfeiture shall be
53 held to be waived by any requirement or proceeding on the part
54 of this Company relating to appraisal or to any examination
55 provided for herein.
56 **Cancellation**   This policy shall be cancelled at any time
57 **of policy.**   at the request of the insured, in which case
58   this Company shall, upon demand and sur-
59 render of this policy, refund the excess of paid premium above

98

60 the customary short rates for the expired time. This pol-
61 icy may be cancelled at any time by this Company by giving
62 to the insured a five days' written notice of cancellation with
63 or without tender of the excess of paid premium above the pro
64 rata premium for the expired time, which excess, if not ten-
65 dered, shall be refunded on demand. Notice of cancellation shall
66 state that said excess premium (if not tendered) will be re-
67 funded on demand.
68 **Mortgagee**   If loss hereunder is made payable, in whole
69 **interests and**   or in part, to a designated mortgagee not
70 **obligations.**   named herein as the insured, such interest in
71   this policy may be cancelled by giving to such
72   mortgagee a ten days' written notice of can-
73 cellation.
74 If the insured fails to render proof of loss such mortgagee, upon
75 notice, shall render proof of loss in the form herein specified
76 within sixty (60) days thereafter and shall be subject to the pro-
77 visions hereof relating to appraisal and time of payment and of
78 bringing suit. If this Company shall claim that no liability ex-
79 isted as to the mortgagor or owner, it shall, to the extent of pay-
80 ment of loss to the mortgagee, be subrogated to all the mort-
81 gagee's rights of recovery, but without impairing mortgagee's
82 right to sue; or it may pay off the mortgage debt and require
83 an assignment thereof and of the mortgage. Other provisions
84 relating to the interests and obligations of such mortgagee may
85 be added hereto by agreement in writing.
86 **Pro rata liability.**   This Company shall not be liable for a greater
87   proportion of any loss than the amount
88 hereby insured shall bear to the whole insurance covering the
89 property against the peril involved, whether collectible or not.
90 **Requirements in**   The insured shall give immediate written
91 **case loss occurs.** notice to this Company of any loss, protect
92   the property from further damage, forthwith
93 separate the damaged and undamaged personal property, put
94 it in the best possible order, furnish a complete inventory of
95 the destroyed, damaged and undamaged property, showing in
96 detail quantities, costs, actual cash value and amount of loss
97 claimed; **and within sixty days after the loss, unless such time
98 is extended in writing by this Company, the insured shall render
99 to this Company a proof of loss,** signed and sworn to by the
100 insured, stating the knowledge and belief of the insured as to
101 the following: the time and origin of the loss, the interest of the
102 insured and of all others in the property, the actual cash value of
103 each item thereof and the amount of loss thereto, all encum-
104 brances thereon, all other contracts of insurance, whether valid
105 or not, covering any of said property, any changes in the title,
106 use, occupation, location, possession or exposures of said prop-
107 erty since the issuing of this policy, by whom and for what
108 purpose any building herein described and the several parts
109 thereof were occupied at the time of loss and whether or not it
110 then stood on leased ground, and shall furnish a copy of all the
111 descriptions and schedules in all policies and, if required, verified
112 plans and specifications of any building, fixtures or machinery
113 destroyed or damaged. The insured, as often as may be reason-
114 ably required, shall exhibit to any person designated by this
115 Company all that remains of any property herein described, and
116 submit to examinations under oath by any person named by this
117 Company, and subscribe the same; and, as often as may be

118 reasonably required, shall produce for examination all books of
119 account, bills, invoices and other vouchers, or certified copies
120 thereof if originals be lost, at such reasonable time and place as
121 may be designated by this Company or its representative, and
122 shall permit extracts and copies thereof to be made.
123 **Appraisal.**   In case the insured and this Company shall
124   fail to agree as to the actual cash value or
125 the amount of loss, then, on the written demand of either, each
126 shall select a competent and disinterested appraiser and notify
127 the other of the appraiser selected within twenty days of such
128 demand. The appraisers shall first select a competent and dis-
129 interested umpire; and failing for fifteen days to agree upon
130 such umpire, then, on request of the insured or this Company,
131 such umpire shall be selected by a judge of a court of record in
132 the state in which the property covered is located.   The ap-
133 praisers shall then appraise the loss, stating separately actual
134 cash value and loss to each item; and, failing to agree, shall
135 submit their differences, only, to the umpire.   An award in writ-
136 ing, so itemized, of any two when filed with this Company shall
137 determine the amount of actual cash value and loss.   Each
138 appraiser shall be paid by the party selecting him and the ex-
139 penses of appraisal and umpire shall be paid by the parties
140 equally.
141 **Company's**   It shall be optional with this Company to
142 **options.**   take all, or any part, of the property at the
143   agreed or appraised value, and also to re-
144 pair, rebuild or replace the property destroyed or damaged with
145 other of like kind and quality within a reasonable time, on giv-
146 ing notice of its intention so to do within thirty days after the
147 receipt of the proof of loss herein required.
148 **Abandonment.**   There can be no abandonment to this Com-
149   pany of any property.
150 **When loss**   The amount of loss for which this Company
151 **payable.**   may be liable shall be payable sixty days
152   after proof of loss, as herein provided, is
153 received by this Company and ascertainment of the loss is made
154 either by agreement between the insured and this Company ex-
155 pressed in writing or by the filing with this Company of an
156 award as herein provided.
157 **Suit.**   No suit or action on this policy for the recov-
158   ery of any claim shall be sustainable in any
159 court of law or equity unless all the requirements of this policy
160 shall have been complied with, and unless commenced within
161 twelve months next after inception of the loss.
162 **Subrogation.**   This Company may require from the insured
163   an assignment of all right of recovery against
164 any party for loss to the extent that payment therefor is made
165 by this Company.

BIBLIOGRAPHY

AFIPS, *System Review Manual on Security*, Montvale, New Jersey, 1974.

Bjork, L. A., Jr., "Generalized Audit Trail Requirements and Concepts for Data Base Applications," *IBM Systems Journal*, Volume 14, Number 3, 1975.

Browne, Peter S., *Computer Security—A Risk Management Approach*, Computer Security Institute, First Annual Computer Security Conference and Workshop, New York, 1974.

The Diebold Research Program, *Insuring the Security of the Information Resource*, 1971.

FIPS Pub 41, *Computer Security Guidelines for Implementing The Privacy Act of 1974*, vs. Department of Commerce, 1975 (SD Catalog Number C13.52:41).

Gladney, H. M., et al., "An Access Control Mechanism for Computing Resources," *IBM Systems Journal*, Volume 14, Number 3, 1975.

IBM Corporation, *IMS/VS General Information Manual*, GH 20-1260, 1975.

IBM Corporation, *The Considerations of Data Security in a Computer Environment*, G520-2169, 1972.

IBM Corporation, *The Considerations of Physical Security in a Computer Environment*, G520-2700, 1970.

IBM Corporation, *Resource Access Control Facility (RACF)*, G520-3081, 1976.

Martin, J., *Security Accuracy and Privacy in Computer Systems*, Englewood Cliffs, New Jersey, Prentice-Hall, 1973.

Packer, Donn B., et al., *Computer Abuse*, California; Stanford Research Institute, 1973 (prepared for the National Science Foundation, RANN NSF7FA/s-73-017, Under Grant GI-37226).

Short, G. F., *Establishing a Company Security Program*, IBM Data Security Forum, Denver, 1974.

Wasserman, J. J., "Data Security in an On-line Computer Environment," *The EDP Auditor*, 1974.

INDEX